The Supreme Court

ITS POLITICS, PERSONALITIES,
AND PROCEDURES

——— The Supreme Court

ITS POLITICS, PERSONALITIES, AND PROCEDURES

John R. Schmidhauser, STATE UNIVERSITY OF IOWA

HOLT, RINEHART AND WINSTON
NEW YORK · CHICAGO · SAN FRANCISCO
TORONTO · LONDON

January, 1967

to my parents

Preface

SINCE 1937, the Supreme Court of the United States has been subjected to a series of attacks perhaps more unrelenting than those which were directed against the "Nine Old Men" of the earlier 1930's. The modern attacks are directed not only to the substance of the Supreme Court's decisions but also against the justices, their law clerks, and the very manner in which the Court operates as a working institution. This book is concerned primarily with aspects of the problem that are ordinarily omitted in the constitutional law casebook—the realities of the judicial selection process, the relationship of the Supreme Court to the state supreme courts and to professional legal organizations, and the evolution and modern characteristics of the decision-making process, each topic being treated in historical perspective.

The book is intended for several uses: as a supplement to American government texts or constitutional law casebooks in political science courses; as a supplement to materials offered in courses on modern American history; and as a work which may be of value to state or federal judges, lawyers, and interested laymen.

Because the data-gathering stage of this slim volume began more than four years ago, my indebtedness extends to many individuals. Several of my colleagues at the State University of Iowa, notably Vernon Van Dyke, Lane Davis, Donald B. Johnson, Arnold Rogow, and Samuel Hays (History), read portions of the manuscript and gave helpful advice and encouragement. Chester Bain of the University of Virginia aided not only in this respect, but also, at crucial junctures, in the gathering of data. Devere Pentony, Merle Arp, and Eugene Reyhons were of invaluable assistance in gathering material for the chapter on the backgrounds of the justices.

The State University of Iowa provided a semester under its research professorship program. Mrs. Marilyn Christensen of Iowa City and Mrs. Carole Finlayson of Chicago provided expert typing assistance. After completion of the final draft of the manuscript, Professor Roger Cramton, former law clerk to Justice Harold Burton and presently a member of the faculty of the Law School of the University of Chicago, critically appraised the chapters dealing with the internal operation of the Supreme Court. Professor Joseph Tanenhaus of the Department of Government of New York University read critically the entire manuscript. Both saved me from some errors of fact. However, I am afraid that the combined wisdom of all the readers was not enough to save me from what some may consider errors of judgment. Neither the State University of Iowa nor the editorial readers can be held responsible for the positions taken or conclusions drawn in this study.

J. R. S.

Chicago, Illinois
April, 1960

——— Contents

—— I

The Realities of Judicial Selection

——— 1

Introduction

ONE OF THE MOST significant trends in the study and teaching of American political institutions in recent years has been the increasing attention devoted to government as a dynamic process rather than as a formal legalistic structure. However, this emphasis upon dynamics has extended, by and large, only to the executive and legislative branches of American government. With a few conspicuous exceptions,[1] academic treatment of the American judiciary has generally retained its traditional orientation.

The staple in American constitutional law for many years has been the casebook containing a collection of excerpts from important Supreme Court decisions. The superior constitutional law casebooks contain excellently written introductory essays which provide a concise historical analysis of the social and legal problems faced by the Supreme Court in the decisions reproduced therein. The focus of intellectual attention in these casebooks has been primarily upon *what* the Supreme Court has decided, *why* such decisions were made, and, when prepared for a liberal arts college, *what* significance these decisions may have for American constitutional development.

As an educational device, the constitutional law casebook fills a vital need in the liberal arts college and may be expected to continue to fill this need in the future. However, the conventional casebook is not ordinarily concerned with the kind of studies or problems that may contribute to understanding the federal Supreme Court as a working institution. Specifically, such understanding may be gained through attempts at answering questions of the following kind: *how* and *why* are particular men chosen to serve on the Court, *what* manner of men are so chosen, *how* does the Supreme Court actually make its decisions (its internal procedures and customs), and *how* does the Supreme Court operate in its administrative relations with other political institutions such as Congress, the President, the Budget Bureau, the Department of Justice, the inferior federal courts, and the state judicial systems? It is with some of the hows and whys of judicial selection and operation that this study is primarily concerned. Special attention is given to the problems of selection and internal operation which have been centers of controversy since 1937.

Over a quarter of a century ago, Felix Frankfurter and James M. Landis presented a powerful intellectual argument for such studies when they pointed out that "the formalities and modes of doing business, which we characterize as procedure, though lacking in dramatic manifestations, may, like the subtle creeping in of the tide, be a powerful force in the dynamic process of government." [2]

The shift in emphasis in this study is not limited to substance but extends to questions of method as well. Without eschewing the very useful and necessary techniques of historical analysis and biographical interpretation that have influenced teaching and writing in constitutional law in the past three decades, this study is also designed to apply where possible the modern techniques of political sociology to the study of the Supreme Court.

Concerning the ambivalence of men toward the goal of achievement of ideal justice, Brooks Adams once wrote,

> Taking the human race collectively, its ideal of a court of justice has been the omniscient and inexorable judgment seat of God. Individually, on the other hand, they have dearly loved favor. . . . The whole development of civilization may be followed in the oscillation of any given society between these two extremes, the many always striving to so restrain the judiciary that it shall be unable to work the will of the favored few. [3]

Lest the chapters that follow be considered simply a series of irreverent attempts at demolishing conceptions of judicial impartiality and long-cherished belief in the attainability of ideal justice, it should be remembered that ideals may scarcely aspire to fulfillment through mere camouflage of the political and ideological realities. The ultimate objective is not to debunk but to understand. In seeking to understand, one must explore the developments in American society which have conditioned contemporary attitudes toward the Supreme Court as an institution as well as toward the Court's decision-making policies. In this context, the assessments of the impact of McCarthyism and of the bitter regional reaction to *Brown* v. *Board of Education* perhaps do not fully explain the contemporary Court crisis. Neither do they fully explain the reasons for the general professional coolness toward the Warren Court, a coolness perceptively described by the New York Supreme Court Justice Samuel Hofstadter in the following manner:

> The failure of lawyers—generally—[both] Bench and Bar—to defend the United States Supreme Court against almost incredible vituperation, and their own intemperate criticism because of recent civil liberties decisions, is greatly disturbing.[4]

References

1. See, for example, Jack W. Peltason, *Federal Courts in the Political Process* (Garden City, N.Y.: Doubleday & Company, Inc., 1955).

2. Felix Frankfurter and James M. Landis, *The Business of the Supreme Court* (New York: The Macmillan Company, 1927), p. vi.

3. Brooks Adams, *The Theory of Social Revolutions* (New York: The Macmillan Company, 1913), p. 36.

4. Letter (October, 1958), *44 American Bar Association Journal* (1958), 920, 928.

2

Politics and the Methods of Selecting Judges

ALTHOUGH THE characterization of the American political system as a "government of laws, not men" has value as a myth which emphasizes the ideal of impartial justice, it has never been satisfactory as a literal description of the political process. Laws are made, enforced, and interpreted by men. The interpretation of laws, constitutional and statutory, by the Supreme Court bears the indelible stamp of the men who serve on this Court. Similarly, the internal procedures and customs of the Supreme Court reflect the characteristics, purposes, and desires of these men. Consequently, the question what manner of men become justices is of crucial importance in the analysis of the Supreme Court as a dynamic institution.

The characteristics of the men chosen for the Supreme Court are determined by a variety of factors, the more important of which include the method of judicial selection and the social and political conditions influencing such selection in America. The latter will be treated in Chapter 3. In this chapter, the origin and characteristics of the method of selection of Supreme Court members will first be discussed. Secondly, this selection method will be analyzed in the light of several propositions concerning the improvement of judicial personnel at all levels of judicial administration, federal, state, and local. Thirdly, major post-World War II developments concerning the federal judicial selection efforts of groups external to the federal government will be discussed and evaluated.

6

The Origin of the Contemporary Method of Selecting Supreme Court Members

Like many other items in the federal Constitution, the choice of a method of selection of members of the Supreme Court was the result of a series of compromises. Initially, the Randolph Plan of Union, which was the first presented to the Philadelphia Convention, provided for appointment by the "National legislature." [1] During the early days of the Convention, only one alternative was suggested, that of appointment by the executive alone. Members of the Convention apparently became so tense and antagonistic in their discussions of this issue that by June 5, 1787, Benjamin Franklin, in his role as elder statesman and peacemaker, felt it necessary to suggest to the Convention that the two modes of judicial selection thus far debated did not exhaust the possibilities. In Madison's description,

> He [Franklin] then in a brief and entertaining manner related a Scotch mode, in which the nomination proceeded from the Lawyers, who always selected the ablest of the profession in order to get rid of him, and share his practice among themselves. It was here he said the interest of the electors to make the best choice, which should always be the case if possible.[2]

There is no evidence that Franklin's comment was intended as a serious suggestion. In any event, it was not treated as such and was never debated or discussed by the delegates. It, more likely, was a light remark designed to ease tensions and to remind the delegates of the need to devise a selection method calculated to secure good appointments.

Franklin's reference to the quality of the potential judicial appointees was not the only indication of the Convention's awareness of this objective. However, detailed analysis of the debates and votes concerning the method of appointment of Supreme Court justices indicated that a great deal more attention was given to matters reflecting regional antagonisms or interest-group objectives.[3] Thus while Madison, at one stage of the Convention developments, supported appointment by the Senate alone, and attacked selection of the justices by the national legislature on the ground that individuals so chosen would be lacking in the qualifications requisite for "an expositor of the laws," he later opposed exclusive senatorial appointment because, in tough-minded sectional terms, this method would throw control into the hands of "ye Northern states," and because the Senate was to represent the states equally. Conversely, Luther Martin, a stanch advocate of state sovereignty, supported exclusive appointment by the Senate "because taken from all the states it would be best informed of characters and most capable of making a fit choice." The smug satisfaction evident in this statement undoubtedly reflected his knowledge that the selection of members of the Senate would be on the basis of state equality. The late Senator Langer of North Dakota, who recently urged that the Senate reject all Supreme Court nominations until North Dakota achieved representation on the Court,[4] would have found bitter solace in the prophetic wisdom of convention delegate Bedford of Delaware. For Bedford, reflecting the uneasiness of the delegates from the small states, opposed appointment of the justices exclusively by the executive because "it would put it in his power to gain over the larger states, by gratifying them with a preference of their Citizens."

Among the alternatives seriously considered by the Convention were selection by the national legislature, by the executive alone, by the Senate alone, and finally nomination and appointment by the President with the advice and consent of the Senate, a method modeled after the system used in the state of Massachusetts. By and large the choice of the last-mentioned method was determined by a complex interplay of factors and was inexorably bound up with the major political issues of the Convention—small versus large states, northern versus southern interest, and popular versus aristocratic government. In the opening days of the Convention, selection by both houses of the national legislature seemed to be the preference of a majority. This attitude reflected, however, not so much the approval of the Convention as the fact that this method was part of the Randolph Plan which had the strategic advantage of being the first presented to the Convention. For a long period, June 13 to September 7, selection of justices by the Senate alone was supported by a majority of delegates in the Convention. Not until the closing days of the Convention was the present mode of nomination and appointment, by the President with the advice and consent of the Senate, finally adopted. This method was clearly a product of political compromise. As such it represented one of a series of complex adjustments between contending forces within the Convention. In the debates it was made clear that the framers hoped to establish a system of judicial selection which would place on the Supreme Court men of integrity, impartiality, and high legal ability. Nevertheless, there were also expressed, with candor and realism, opinions which indicated a keen awareness of the geographical and interest-group considerations which have, in fact, influenced the federal judicial appointing process down to the present day.

The text of Article III, section 1, of the Constitution, provides for one Supreme Court and "such inferior courts as the Congress may from time to time ordain and establish." Of the qualifications of the judges and justices nothing was said explicitly. Presumably the criteria for selection were left to the appointing authority, the President, whose nominations were subject to the advice and consent of the Senate. Article II, section 2, refers, incidentally, only to the appointment of "judges of the Supreme Court," although by long practice the same method of selection has been utilized for judges of the inferior federal courts.

Although the setting of explicit or implicit qualifications for the federal justices and judges was left to an appointing authority consisting of the President and the Senate, Congress in its entirety did assume a number of far-reaching responsibilities in the organization of the courts in the Judiciary Act of 1789. Under this act, the Supreme Court was first established as a six-man tribunal, comprised of a Chief Justice and five Associate Justices. Thus Congress asserted the power to determine the size of the Supreme Court, a power which has been of great importance in several historical periods. Furthermore, in Congress' original effort at judicial organization, the size of the Supreme Court was made contingent upon the nature of the inferior federal court system.

The Act of 1789 provided for thirteen judicial districts and an equal number of district judges. The judicial districts were grouped into three judicial circuits corresponding to the three great sectional divisions of the infant republic, Northern (but designated Eastern), which comprised New England and New York; Middle, consisting of Pennsylvania, New Jersey, Delaware, Maryland, and Virginia; and Southern, comprising North and South Carolina and Georgia. Since each circuit court was to be held by two Supreme Court justices and a district judge, the logic of this organization of the inferior federal courts not only influenced the size of the Supreme Court but also implied a system of geographical distribution of Supreme Court appointments.[5]

It is clear that before the first member of the Supreme Court was chosen, the method of judicial selection designated by the constitutional framers and the system of judicial organization established by the first Congress laid the groundwork for a Supreme Court which was to be chosen, at least to a certain extent, on the basis of a number of political considerations. These political considerations included recognition of the qualitative characteristics, ideological predilections, interest-group affiliations and sectional backgrounds of potential justices.

Efforts to Change Formally the Mode of Selection

In the many decades since 1789, several suggestions for alteration in the mode of choosing members of the Supreme Court have been made. On one occasion, an attempt was made to give the House of Representatives a voice in the appointing process equal to that of the Senate. This effort was made by Senator Hillhouse of Connecticut in 1808. Three attempts were made to vest the judicial appointment power solely in the two legislative houses, the first by Congressman Lewis of Virginia in 1818 and the remainder by Congressman Cobb of Wisconsin in 1867 and 1868.[6] All of these efforts were in the form of proposed constitutional amendments and all were manifestations of congressional and presidential rivalry over the Supreme Court selection process.

In the period 1889–1926, no fewer than thirteen proposed constitutional amendments were introduced in Congress which provided for the popular election of members of the Supreme Court. In eleven of these, the associate justices were to be chosen by the electors of the circuit in which the justices would serve, while the Chief Justice was to be elected at large. In the remaining two proposals, all the Court members were to be elected in their respective circuits. The Chief Justice was to be elected by the Court members from their number.[7] These amendments were part of the widespread Progressive attempts at making the state and federal judiciaries more responsive to the will of the people.

Scattered attempts at changing the mode of selecting Supreme Court members have been made in the period since 1926 both in the form of proposed constitutional amendments [8] and in proposed legislative enactments. The most recent was embodied in a bill introduced by Senator Smathers of Florida which would require of all appointees to the Supreme Court five years prior judicial experience either on an inferior federal court or upon the highest court of a state.[9]

None of the formally proposed changes in the method of selection of Supreme Court members achieved success or gained widespread public support. The American public has generally rejected open and aboveboard attempts at changing the federal judicial system, whether these attempts were directed at the Supreme Court's jurisdiction or against the selection arrangements. Yet how has American democracy fared in coping with more quiet and subtle efforts at ideological control of the Supreme Court by political parties, factions within political parties, and especially private groups? This question will be dealt with first in terms of the role of the Senate in confirming presidential selections to the Supreme Court and in terms of the seemingly related custom of senatorial courtesy, and, secondly, with respect to the objectives and techniques of private-interest groups with particular emphasis upon the organized bar.

The Role of the Senate in Supreme Court Selection

The ideological influences which were brought to bear in the judicial selection process and the importance of the Senate in this process are discussed in greater detail in Chapter 3. Nevertheless, the impact of these factors deserves brief consideration in the context of this assessment of selection methods. It is certainly apparent that the ideological attitudes held by or attributed to candidates for nomination and appointment to the Supreme Court represented the most important factor influencing presidential choice. Conversely, where a majority of the Senate entertained ideological assumptions contradicting those of a weak president, on a number of historical occasions, such Senate majorities succeeded in rejecting presidential nominees. Senatorial influence in such situations was essentially negative, but nonetheless effective.[10]

It should be added that the Senate's power to thwart appointments to the Supreme Court differs considerably from its power virtually to choose, through the medium of senatorial courtesy, judges of the inferior federal tribunals. The power of individual members of the Senate is generally inadequate to influence presidential choice of Supreme Court members. Even on the rare occasions when a majority of the Senate combines against a nominee for the Supreme bench, the effect is a negative one, preventing a particular selection, rather than positively designating a nominee and forcing his choice upon the President.[11] With respect to appointments to the inferior federal courts, individual senators of the same party as the President may wield decisive influence. Furthermore, where the senatorial seats in a state are held by senators of the party in opposition to the President, such influence may devolve upon the state chairman of the President's political party.[12] In practical effect, the choice of a federal judge may often be a senator's rather than the President's. The considerations governing a senator in such a selection often are of primarily local or regional significance, while in contrast, the presidential choice of a member of the Supreme Court involves or should involve far more complex considerations.

It is clear that the choice of a method of judicial selection, whether for the Supreme Court of the United States or the inferior federal courts, has often become the focus of intense ideological partisanship. While the establishment of the custom of senatorial courtesy has altered the method of selection of inferior federal judges, the method of nominating and appointing Supreme Court justices has remained, as intended by the constitutional framers, a prerogative of the President. It would, of course, be a mistake to conclude that because senatorial courtesy has had little influence in the process of selection of Supreme Court members, the process is free from political and ideological influences. Quite the contrary, political and ideological influences of the strongest sort are normally present when a justice is chosen by a president. The basic difference concerns the nature of these influences. Presidential domination of the selection process usually entails political and ideological considerations which may be relevant to a national, more heterogeneous constituency rather than to the frequently narrow, more parochial concerns of a senator.

A president is nevertheless subject to pressures which emanate from private groups which, though national in their organizational attributes, may be excessively narrow and self-serving in their public policy objectives. The determined efforts of railroad magnates, such as Leland Stanford, to influence the judicial selections of a number of Presidents in the last half of the nineteenth century illustrate this. Powerful interest groups also tend to concentrate their efforts upon members of the Senate Judiciary Committee who may be sympathetic to them. This tactic assumes great importance to interest groups that may find themselves out of favor at the White House. In such circumstances the more aggressive groups may concentrate intensive efforts upon the Committee members in order to defeat presidential nominees considered ideologically unsound or unfriendly. Thus conservative groups vigorously, but unsuccessfully, opposed Louis D. Brandeis while, conversely, groups such as organized labor and the National Association for the Advancement of Colored People successfully opposed Judge John J. Parker.[13] In both instances the opposition concentrated its greatest efforts upon the Senate Judiciary Committee.

The tendency for interest groups to attempt to influence federal judicial selection has, of course, long been characteristic of American politics. In the contemporary era, the role of the organized bar has assumed special significance because of the widespread success of the American Bar Association at the federal as well as state levels. This success may, in part, reflect the temper of the times as well as the Association's consistency of interest and purpose and its claim of special competence in matters concerning judicial selection and administration. In any event, the contemporary successes of the Association warrant an appraisal of the objectives and methods of the organized bar and an assessment of the possible significance of these successes for the federal judicial system.

The Objectives and Methods of the American Bar Association

Since the program of the American Bar Association concerned with the selection of Supreme Court justices is closely related to the efforts of the organized bar at influencing judicial selection at every level of judicial activity whether federal or state, it would seem useful, by way of introduction, to treat the general objectives and methods of the state bar associations as well as the national association. The bar associations, both state and national, have concerned themselves with judicial selection in the federal, state, and local courts for decades. In 1928, for example, the Committee on Judicial Selection of the American Bar Association commented with satisfaction upon the "sustained effort . . . through the state and local bar associations . . . [which] will in due course of time serve to stamp the system of judicial selection through the medium of the Bar as an accepted institution in our political life— accepted by the people, we mean—with the like force of law itself." [14] The intensity of association activities in these matters is demonstrated by the fact that in 1932 association efforts to influence judicial selection were made in all but two of the cities with a population of 450,000 or more, and in 27 of the 42 cities having a population of 200,000 or more.[15]

The viewpoint of the leadership of the American Bar Association on matters of this kind is abundantly clear. The Association feels that lawyers have unique competence in such matters. The *American Bar Association Journal* stated recently that "because lawyers are the only group of citizens that are in daily contact with the courts, they are the only group that are really able to judge the qualifications necessary for good judicial material." [16] Because of the missionary fervor and growing success of the Association in influencing federal judicial appointments, including those to the Supreme Court, the objectives and potential consequences of such influence should be thoroughly explored. What criteria are applied by the bar associations in determining good judicial appointees?

Politics and the Selection of "Good" Judges

In recent years, the American Bar Association and a number of academicians have given a great deal of attention to the determination of the most effective method of selecting good federal and state judges.[17] The meaning of the word "good" is of course the key factor to be analyzed. If one were to take at face value the numerous, and frequently repetitive, discussions of judicial selection in the journals of the American Bar Association and the American Judicature Society, one would conclude that impartiality, based upon honesty, competence, intelligence, and sound legal training, is universally accepted as the hallmark of the good judge. Conversely, "politics" in the selection process is generally condemned as the most baneful of possible influences.[18] There is, however, considerable evidence to indicate that the leaders of the bar may, under the façade of reformation of the courts, occasionally be more interested in the ideological assumptions of judicial candidates than in the ideal of impartiality.

This point may be clarified by sharply distinguishing partisan politics in its narrower context and ideological partisanship of a broader and more persuasive character. Undoubtedly, increased bar association influence in judicial selection might reduce the importance of party labels. But politics or partisanship takes many forms and frequently includes considerations such as basic assumptions about the rights or duties of owners of private property or the virtues of maintaining rural rather than urban dominance in politics which in many situations defy definition under regular party labels. Politics in modern American parlance may have, as

Professor Robert Y. Fluno has suggested, four relatively distinct meanings relating to (a) the rewards or punishments of political party organizations; (b) the pressure of public opinion; (c) the broad development of public policy through the governmental process; and (d) the intense competition of aggressive power groups within American society.[19]

The tendency for leaders of the bar consciously or unconsciously to associate criteria relating to the personal qualifications of judicial candidates, such as the previously mentioned attributes of honesty, intelligence, competence, and sound legal training, with their ideological predilections, is amply demonstrated by analysis of the positions taken by leaders of the American Bar Association with respect to several contested selections to the Supreme Court. In addition, analysis of the rationale for proposed changes in judicial selection methods may be instructive.

In an address to the American Political Science Association in 1947, Judge Parker, a recognized protagonist of the Bar Association's point of view, discussed at great length the attributes of good judges, stressing the individual qualities that purportedly contributed to high legal competence and stern impartiality in judicial decision making, and concluding that the appointive method of judicial selection was by far superior to the elective one. Yet in defending this position, Parker, apparently without recognizing the inherent intellectual contradiction, disclosed by implication the ideological basis for his choice—distrust of urban political power. In his words,

> In the rural sections, where the bar has a predominating influence even in political elections, the results of judicial election have not been too bad. With the growth of cities, however, and the rise of the city machine with the decline of the bar in political influence, it is clear that some other method of judicial selection must be employed if the high character of the bench of America is to be maintained.[20]

As a matter of fact, the observation of Professor Willard Hurst that "bar activity in judicial elections was definitely an urban phenomenon"[21] may, upon close investigation, be primarily a manifestation of the bar's satisfaction with the ideology of rural political leaders, rather than a desire to improve the caliber of judicial candidates. This remark does not imply that the urban bar associations lack bases for seeking to correct abuses of judicial power, but it is not at all clear that interest in the quality of judicial selections overshadowed ideological considerations.

Perhaps one of the clearest illustrations of the tendency to confuse ideology and legal competence is provided by the views of William Howard Taft on judicial selection. Despite the fact that he served long periods in federal executive posts, including those of Civil Governor of the Philippine Islands, Secretary of War, and the Presidency, Taft viewed with most satisfaction his judicial and legal career. Taft had served as a state judge, a federal circuit judge, a law professor, and finally as Chief Justice of the United States. He was for many years one of the most influential leaders of the American Bar Association, serving as its president and heading the Association committee which formulated the Canons of Judicial Ethics. The Canons contain the very standards of legal ability, personal integrity, and intellectual impartiality which the Association has advocated in its judicial selection efforts for over a quarter of a century.

The formulation and adoption of these criteria owed a great deal to the personal efforts of Taft. Yet in 1916 the same Taft signed, with six other former presidents of the American Bar Association,[22] the statement submitted to the Senate Judiciary Committee that "taking into consideration the reputation, character, and professional career of Mr. Louis D. Brandeis, he is not a fit person to be a member of the Supreme Court of the United States." [23] The real basis for the opposition of the bar leaders was not the fitness of Brandeis, but his lack of sympathy for the values which they cherished. As Taft expressed it in a private letter,

> . . . it is one of the deepest wounds that I have had as an American and a lover of the Constitution and a believer in progressive conservatism that such a man as Brandeis would be put in the court. . . . He is a muckraker, an emotionalist for his own purposes, a Socialist. . . .[24]

The high and objective standards for judicial selection which Taft himself had helped establish for the American Bar Association were overshadowed by passionate ideological partisanship.

Nor was this the only instance of this kind in Taft's career. During the heat of the presidential election campaign of 1920, Taft, from his sanctuary at Yale University, intervened in behalf of the Republican candidate, Warren G. Harding. Taft, in opposing Harding's Democratic opponent, James Cox, did not question Cox's ability to choose justices who were competent legally, honest personally, or qualified by professional training. As he had done in 1916, Taft let the cat out of the bag by ignoring these objective standards for judicial selection and by emphasizing the underlying ideological reasons for his opposition to Cox. Wrote Taft in the October, 1920, issue of the *Yale Review:*

> Mr. Wilson is in favor of a latitudinarian construction of the Constitution of the United States, to weaken the protection it should afford against Socialist raids upon property rights. . . .
>
> He had made three appointments to the Supreme Court. He is understood to be greatly disappointed in the attitude of the first of these [Mr. Justice McReynolds] upon such questions. The other two [Mr. Justice Brandeis and Mr. Justice Clarke] represent a new school of constitutional construction, which, if allowed to prevail, will greatly impair our fundamental law. Four of the incumbent Justices are beyond the retirement age of seventy, and the next President will probably be called upon to appoint their successors. There is no greater domestic issue in this election than the maintenance of the Supreme Court as the bulwark to enforce the guarantee that no man shall be deprived of his property without due process of law. . . .[25]

Ironically, another example of the underlying ideological partisanship which has, on occasion, influenced judicial selection recommendations by leaders of the organized bar is provided by the nomination of Tom Clark in 1949. Clark's nomination was strongly opposed by liberal and left-wing groups and by John L. Lewis and the United Mine Workers. Of Clark's qualifications for an associate justiceship, the *Washington Post* had commented, acidly, that his name would not have been found on a "list of distinguished jurists such as a conscientious President usually assembles before making an appointment to the Supreme Court." [26] However, four former presidents of the American Bar Association and a large number of presidents of state and local bar associations strongly supported Clark.[27] The reason for such support seems clearly a matter of Clark's ideological conservatism; his qualifications for high judicial office were of secondary importance. The contrast between the treatment of Brandeis and that of Clark by bar leaders is a telling one.

The realistic possibility that the leaders of the bar may attempt in the future to enforce their private brand of ideological conformity under the guise of selecting "good" judges and justices represents but one aspect of the problem, for any shift, whether formal or informal, of the authority to select judicial personnel from publicly responsible officials to a private group such as the American Bar Association involves additional dangers. First, the control of judicial selection within the private group very likely would fall into the hands of an active minority. Consequently, in the long run, an elite within an already politically irresponsible private group could determine the ideological prerequisites of membership in the Supreme Court and inferior federal courts. Secondly, the procedures by which candidates for judicial posts would be screened might, since they would be adopted outside the arena of public control and scrutiny, be manifestly unfair or prone to abuses of various kinds.

Concerning the first possibility, it has become virtually a tradition of the American Bar Association that its leaders comprise those who achieved high economic success in the profession and who entertained deeply conservative viewpoints on economic and social questions.[28] These leaders manage the affairs of the Association and set the tone and temper of its activities.

The influence which the Association maintains in the selection of state and federal judges and justices is essentially the influence of this small group of Association leaders. Because of the social and economic background, the group associations, and the social outlook of these Bar Association leaders, such influence has inevitably been sternly conservative in the past [29] and is likely to remain so in the future.[30]

Concerning the possibility that a private group, such as the American Bar Association, might abuse its power to influence judicial selection, the description of the situation in Chicago prior to the mid-1930's is instructive. In an article written in opposition to a plan vesting virtual control of the selection of judges in Cook County, Illinois, in the hands of the Chicago Bar Association, Harry M. Fisher, Chief Justice of the Circuit Court of Cook County, etched the following description of the realities of bar association screening of judicial candidates.

. . . each candidate for judicial office, the sitting judge included, leans upon two supporting props, both political: (1) His party central committee, which under the law nominates him and under our party system has the power to deliver votes, and (2) the Bar Association, which under prevailing custom is the most potent instrument for creating favorable public opinion since, in a large community like ours, the press is the only medium by which such an opinion can be created, and our newspapers generally follow the Bar Association recommendations. . . .

The prevailing method [of the Chicago Bar Association in 1937] of giving or withholding a favorable report on a sitting judge makes it unnecessary for any member of the [Bar Association's] Board of Governors or the Committee on Candidates to seek favor directly from a judge. Each judge knows who will sit in judgment of him before the next bar primary. Every president of the Bar Association, upon expiration of his term of office, becomes a life member of that committee. . . .

The public gets the impression that the result of a bar primary is the considered verdict of the entire bar, whereas less than twenty-five hundred out of the twelve thousand lawyers in Cook County register their votes in any such primary, and many of these usually have axes to grind. But even these votes are largely inspired by previous reports. The Committee on Candidates sends out a questionnaire to the members of the Association. One of the questions is: "Do you have confidence in his [the candidate's] integrity?" In the answer no bill of particulars is necessary; the questionnaire is returned by mail unsigned. When the envelopes are opened the answers tabulated, no candidate is permitted to be there or have a representative present. Upon these anonymous letters a judge's character is openly and publicly maligned and he is often convicted of being unfit for judicial office—all without an opportunity to defend himself—without a specific charge against him—without a known witness. . . .[31]

The successful opposition of the American Bar Association's Committee on the Judiciary to the candidacy of Congressman Benjamin Rabin to a federal district judgeship in 1947 exemplifies another possibility for abuse. This situation occurred after the death in November, 1946, of District Judge Samuel J. Mandelbaum. The ABA Committee on the Judiciary threw its support behind Harold R. Medina and opposed Rabin on the ground that he was the candidate of Ed Flynn's Democratic organization in the Bronx. The ABA's efforts were successful. Medina was nominated by President Truman and approved by the Senate.[32] But it is noteworthy that in the intensity of its opposition to Rabin as an alleged "political" candidate, the ABA Committee did not bother to consider whether he was qualified for the federal judgeship. Moreover, the November, 1950, edition of the *American Bar Association Journal* carried a guest editorial which commented on Rabin as follows:

> On the recommendation of the political powers of New York, a party follower in Congress was nominated to fill a vacancy in New York. *There were no judicial qualifications of the appointee.* The New York State Bar Association, the Bar Association of the City of New York, the American Bar Association registered emphatic objections. The Judiciary Committee of the Senate was then controlled by the Republicans. When the quality of the appointment was revealed, it was apparent that confirmation was not possible and the appointment was withdrawn.[33]

Rabin objected to the guest editorial and finally, in February, 1952, elicited the following extended apology in the "Editor to Readers" section of the *American Bar Association Journal:*

> The Gentleman referred to [Rabin] has pointed out to us that he could be positively identified from what was said. *The fact is that he was never nominated for the position in question* and therefore the statement that he was nominated to fill the vacancy is not correct. *It is also a fact that his judicial qualifications were not*

passed upon, therefore the statement that he had none is a mis-statement. . . .

In the fall of 1947, he [Rabin] was nominated for Justice of the State Supreme Court. . . . That was the first and only time that his qualifications for judicial office were passed upon. The Association of the Bar of the City of New York then said that he was "well qualified" for the office of Justice of the New York Supreme Court, and the New York County Lawyers Association said he was highly qualified.[34]

While this public apology sufficed with respect to the errors made in the guest editorial of November, 1950, it is noteworthy that nothing was said directly about the fact that the ABA strongly opposed Rabin's candidacy for the federal district judgeship in 1947. Such strong opposition without even cursory evaluation of his judicial qualifications would seem a far greater injustice than the erroneous guest editorial.

The Contemporary Problem

The public policy objectives of the American Bar Association which are discussed in Chapter 4 have particular relevance to the study of the federal Supreme Court because of the increased attention this group has focused upon federal judicial selection since World War II. Although the Association has concerned itself with state and municipal judicial selection since the early 1920's, formal organizational intervention at the federal level began only in 1946. A Committee on Federal Judicial Selection was created by the ABA House of Delegates.[35] By 1947 this Committee was empowered to propose the nomination of "good" lawyers rather than merely to oppose "bad" ones.[36] The Association has sought to establish a system through contacts with the Attorney General, the Senate Judiciary Committee, and the President whereby all presidential nominations for federal judicial appointments are submitted for Association approval or disapproval. In addition, the ABA House of Delegates in 1951 requested the Platform Committees of the Democratic and Republican parties to adopt planks formally requiring the President to consult with the ABA Committee on

Judicial Selection with respect to future nominations.[37] In 1958 the House of Delegates adopted a resolution urging that federal judicial nominations be made by an "independent" commission.[38] Such a commission, similar to those adopted in a few states, would in fact ensure American Bar Association control of the federal judicial selection process.

It is interesting to note that the arguments for increased bar influence in federal judicial selection differ from those offered with respect to the state courts. In terms of the latter, it is argued that a change should be made from the elective to the appointive system. Yet the bar groups find the present appointive federal system unsatisfactory because "politics" is involved. These arguments have, of course, an underlying consistency in that they are predicated upon the assumption that the bar would wield decisive influence as a result of either of the suggested changes.

Should such arrangements become permanently established, it would entail a basic change in the American constitutional system, for it would further modify the explicit grant of constitutional power to the President to nominate and, by and with the advice and consent of the Senate, appoint such judicial personnel. With respect to appointments to inferior federal courts, it would alter the long-established custom of senatorial courtesy whereby, in practical effect, the President's power to nominate may be actually exercised, or at least thwarted, by the senators from the state from which a nominee is selected (if the senators are of the same party as the President). In addition, political circumstances sometimes dictate a selection by the state chairman of the President's political party in the event that the senators from the nominee's state are members of the party in opposition to the President. These arrangements would also be changed by bar selection of judicial personnel. All of these existing arrangements, whether constitutional or customary in origin, have, of course, been criticized because choice under these methods has necessarily involved political considerations of a wide variety.

Yet, although "politics" in judicial selection is condemned as evil, it should be noted that what the bar groups essentially suggest is a substitution of the sort of partisan ideological influences which may be dominant in the affairs of the organized bar associations for the partisan ideological influences which prevail in political parties at the state or national level. This statement does not mean to reject as unworthy the frequently constructive work of bar groups to improve the quality of judicial personnel, but to underscore the dangers inherent in vesting virtual control of judicial selection in politically irresponsible private groups which may on occasion allow partisan ideological considerations to color or overshadow objective criteria for the evaluation of judicial candidates.

Blatant attempts at ideological control of the courts, whether the state courts, the inferior federal tribunals, or the federal Supreme Court, have normally been fiercely rejected by the public. However, the judicial selection plans of the bar associations have achieved some notable successes without ordinarily being subjected to widespread public scrutiny. With respect to efforts at influencing the selection of federal Supreme Court members, the public has had an opportunity to consider the desirability or undesirability of the Smathers bill, which limits choice to candidates who have served five years on an inferior federal court or the highest court of a state.[39] But the selection plan of the American Bar Association regarding the Supreme Court of the United States has not been submitted for wide public discussion and subsequent approval or disapproval, although it has been treated frankly in Association meetings and in the columns of the Association's *Journal*.[40]

In recent years the American Bar Association has succeeded in gaining the approval of President Eisenhower for informal consideration of the qualifications of nominees for the Supreme Court of the United States by the Bar Association. Edward J. Fox, Jr., for some years a member of the Association's Federal Judiciary Committee, gave the following account of the establishment of this arrangement.

> When Chief Justice Vinson died the services of the [Bar Association's] Committee were offered to the Attorney General but the Committee was told that the appointment of a Justice to the Supreme Court was a personal appointment of the President and that if the help of the Committee was needed it would be consulted.

When the next vacancy occurred, the Committee was not consulted, but the Chairman of the Committee was invited by the Deputy Attorney General to testify before the Senate Committee in favor of the confirmation of Judge Harlan.

Deputy Attorney General Rogers, speaking in Baltimore before the regional meeting of the Association in October, 1956, said that when Mr. Justice Brennan's name was discussed with the President, he asked what the American Bar Association Committee thought about him. When he was told that the Committee had not been asked for its opinion, he directed that the nomination be held up until the Committee could report.[41]

The implications of this establishment of bar association influence in the selection of Supreme Court members are many. The permanence or impermanence of this arrangement is, of course, a matter for determination by subsequent presidents.

In the late 1950's, the Supreme Court has been under the heavy criticism of two groups, those who seek to undo racial integration, or at least prevent further pro-integration decisions, and those who view with profound alarm recent Court rulings which have abated the excesses of the guardians of internal security at both the federal and state level. The Supreme Court's decision in *Pennsylvania* v. *Nelson*,[42] in particular, has deprived those ferreting out subversion at the state level of much of the power and, to many, the glory of such pursuits. Because of the successes of men like Senators James Eastland, William Jenner, and John Marshall Butler within the Senate Judiciary Committee and the Senate as a whole in focusing criticism upon the Court [43] the pressure on the Supreme Court in the late 1950's has been likened to the crisis of 1937. Yet, despite the wildness of the contemporary attacks, perhaps it is not too much to suggest that the more sophisticated efforts of the American Bar Association to influence judicial selection may, in the long run, have the greater impact upon the ideology of the Supreme Court.

Conclusions

It is clear that the choice of a method of judicial selection, whether for the Supreme Court of the United States or for lesser courts, has often become not only the focus of intense ideological partisanship but also on occasion a manifestation of such partisanship. A number of publicly sponsored changes in the mode of selecting Supreme Court members have been made since the adoption of the present method in the Philadelphia Convention of 1787. The proposed changes usually took the form of proposed constitutional amendments, although the most recent one introduced by Senator Smathers is in the nature of a proposed legislative enactment. Although they have engendered widespread discussion, the various publicly sponsored proposals never achieved success.

In the realm of political party development, the establishment of the custom of senatorial courtesy often seriously curtailed presidential nominating and appointing authority with respect to appointments to the inferior federal courts. The selection of justices of the Supreme Court has, except for a few situations, remained largely under the control of the President. Consequently, the choice of Supreme Court members has generally reflected the catholic political and ideological considerations of a national constituency, rather than those of a region, state, or congressional district.

Perhaps the most successful of the modern attempts at modifying the method of selection of Supreme Court members has been the quiet effort of the American Bar Association to establish bar influence as a substitute for the allegedly pernicious influence of "politics." This effort is part of the nation-wide attempts by bar groups to influence judicial selection at every level of government —federal, state, and local.

In their public utterances, the leaders of the bar are noted for their reverence for the founding fathers and the principles of government which were adopted in the Philadelphia Convention of 1787. It is therefore curious that modern spokesmen of the legal profession often prefer to ignore the deliberations of the Convention on judicial selection. This lack of interest in the deliberations of the Philadelphia Convention is perhaps explicable because these debates represent one of the clearest examples of the politics of choosing methods of judicial selection. In the contemporary setting the greatest dangers inherent in private-group determination of the qualifications of nominees to the Supreme Court lay in the possibility of the substitution of the ideological prerequisites of a politically irresponsible private group for those of a nationally elected and publicly responsible President.

These background developments underscore the importance of the mode of judicial selection in the American judicial system in general, and the Supreme Court in particular. In order to assess the quality of the judicial appointees, it is necessary not only to analyze the selection practices and objectives of those who share or seek to share the appointing authority, but also to evaluate the characteristics of the judicial appointees themselves.

References

1. Max Farrand (ed.), *The Records of the Federal Convention of 1787* (New Haven, Conn.: Yale University Press, 1911), pp. 21–22.

2. *Ibid.*, pp. 119–120.

3. For the major developments in the Convention respecting judicial selection, see *ibid.*, I, 21, 63, 67, 70, 116, 119–120, 126–128, 224, 232–233, 238, 292; II, 37–38, 41–44, 71–72, 80–83, 183, 383, 389, 394, 495, 537–540, 598, and 627.

4. See the comment on Senator Langer's proposal in *45 American Bar Association Journal* (1959), 762.

5. For a detailed analysis of the relation of Supreme Court appointments and the organization of inferior federal courts in the Judiciary Act of 1789 and in subsequent judiciary acts, see Floyd E. McCaffree, "The Nomination and Confirmation of Justices of the Supreme Court of the United States, 1789–1849" (Unpublished Doctoral dissertation, University of Michigan, 1938).

6. Herman V. Ames, *The Proposed Amendments to the Constitution of the United States during the First Century of Its History.* H.R. Doc., Vol. 74, Part 2, 54th Cong., 2nd Sess. (1896–1897), pp. 146–147.

7. M. A. Musmanno, *Proposed Amendments to the Constitution* (1889–1926). H.R. Doc. No. 551, 70th Cong., 2nd Sess. (1929), p. 86.

8. See Felton M. Johnston, *Proposed Amendments to the Constitution of the United States Introduced in Congress from the 69th Congress, 2nd Session, through the 84th Congress, 2nd Session* (December, 1926, to January 3, 1957). Sen. Doc. No. 65, 85th Cong., 1st Sess. (1957).

9. Cong. Rec., 84th Cong., 2nd Sess., April 30, 1956, p. 6521. The Smathers proposal is discussed in Chapter 3 of this book, pp. 51–54.

10. See Chapter 3 of this book, pp. 47–51.

11. See especially Joseph P. Harris, *The Advice and Consent of the Senate* (Berkeley: University of California Press, 1953), pp. 302–324; also Edward J. Fox, Jr., "The Selection of Federal Judges: The Work of the Federal Judiciary Committee," *43 American Bar Association Journal* (1957), 685–688, 761–764.

12. Fox, *loc. cit.*, p. 687.

13. Harris, *op. cit.*, pp. 99–114, 127–132.

14. "Report of the Committee on Judicial Selection," *14 American Bar Association Journal* (1928), 617.

15. Willard Hurst, *The Growth of American Law: The Law Makers* (Boston: Little, Brown & Company, 1950), p. 130.

16. From the editorial introduction to Fox, *loc. cit.*, p. 685.

17. See especially Arthur T. Vanderbilt, *Judges and Jurors: Their Functions, Qualifications and Selection* (Boston: Boston University Press, 1956), pp. 27–31.

18. Fox, *loc. cit.*, p. 687; see also, Loyd Wright of the American Bar Association, in Jack W. Peltason, *Federal Courts in the Political Process* (Garden City, N.Y.: Doubleday & Company, Inc., 1955), p. 33.

19. Robert Y. Fluno, "How Deep Is the Supreme Court in Politics?" *10 Western Political Quarterly* (1957), 459–461.

20. John J. Parker, "The Judicial Office in the United States," *23 New York University Law Quarterly Review* (1948), 227–229, 234.

21. Hurst, *op. cit.*, p. 130.

22. Elihu Root, Joseph H. Choate, Moorfield Storey, Simeon E. Baldwin, Francis Rawle, and Peter W. Meldrim.

23. Quoted in Alpheus Thomas Mason, *Brandeis: A Free Man's Life* (New York: The Viking Press, 1946), p. 489.

24. Henry F. Pringle, *Life and Times of William Howard Taft*, II (New York: Holt, Rinehart and Winston, Inc., 1939), p. 952.

25. Quoted in Archibald MacLeish and E. F. Prichard, Jr. (eds.), *Law and Politics: Occasional Papers of Felix Frankfurter* (New York: Harcourt, Brace & Company, 1939), p. 37.

26. Quoted in Harris, *op. cit.*, p. 311.

27. *Senate Judiciary Hearings on the nomination of Tom Clark, 81st Cong., 1st Sess.* (1949), pp. 3–29; the former presidents of the American Bar Association were Jacob M. Lashly, Joseph W. Henderson, Willis Smith, and Tappen Gregory.

28. Benjamin R. Twiss, *Lawyers and the Constitution* (Princeton, N.J.: Princeton University Press, 1942), pp. 142–173; Morris Raphael Cohen, *Law and the Social Order* (New York: Harcourt, Brace & Company, 1933), pp. 12–22.

29. The conservatism of the leaders of the American Bar Association has been acknowledged not only by the critics, such as Cohen and Twiss, but by friendly commentators such as M. Louise Rutherford. See especially

her work, *The Influence of the American Bar Association on Public Opinion and Legislation* (Philadelphia: M. Louise Rutherford, 1937), pp. 115–130. The public policy positions of the Association are another reliable indicator; see Chapter 4 of this text, pp. 77–78.

30. The occasional elections to the American Bar Association presidency of moderately liberal individuals such as Whitney Seymour North represent rare exceptions.

31. Harry M. Fisher, "The Selection of Judges for Cook County: The Chicago Bar Association Plan." Reprinted by special permission from the *Illinois Law Review* (Northwestern University School of Law), Volume 31, Number 7, 1937. For a more recent instance in which concern over bar selection or screening of judges was expressed, see Daniel J. Reid's criticism of the Bar Association of the City of New York, in Edith E. Asbury, *New York Times,* February 5, 1960, pp. 1, 20.

32. *33 American Bar Association Journal* (1947), 537–539.

33. Guest Editorial, *36 American Bar Association Journal* (1950), 929–930; italics mine.

34. Editor to Readers, *38 American Bar Association Journal* (1952), 134; italics mine.

35. *32 American Bar Association Journal* (1946), 494.

36. *33 American Bar Association Journal* (1947), 305.

37. Proceedings of the House of Delegates, *37 American Bar Association Journal* (1951), 879.

38. Proceedings of the House of Delegates, *44 American Bar Association Journal* (1958), 1107–1113.

39. Cong. Rec., *loc. cit.,* p. 6521.

40. Fox, *loc. cit.,* pp. 685–688, 761.

41. *Ibid.,* pp. 688, 761.

42. 350 U.S. 497 (1956).

43. See, for example, Anthony Lewis' account of Senate action on legislation designed to curtail the Supreme Court's jurisdiction in certain areas, *New York Times,* August 20, 1958, p. 1.

3

The Social and Political Backgrounds of the Justices of the Supreme Court: 1789-1959 [1]

THE POLITICAL variation on the Horatio Alger theme —any boy, but preferably one of humble origin, may become President—has long been one of the most satisfying of the myths of American political recruitment. This myth has also been applied to national legislative and to other national executive offices. But it is hardly likely that many young men of humble origin have lost sleep contemplating their prospects for attaining a seat on the Supreme Court of the United States. Our highest judicial institution has always been veiled, in the public mind, in an aura of inaccessibility.

Is there any factual basis for popular conceptions of the unlikelihood of appointment to the Supreme Court? A partial explanation is provided by the relative lack of opportunities for such appointment. Since the creation of the Supreme Court, only ninety-two persons have served as members.[2] During the same historical period, literally thousands have served in the national legislature or in high national executive posts. Interestingly enough, the Presidency is considered more accessible than the high bench, even though far fewer individuals have attained the presidential office than have secured appointment to the Supreme Court. The fact that members of the Supreme Court are appointed rather than elected does not account for this distinction. High executive officials at the cabinet level are similarly nominated, and with the consent of the Senate, appointed by the President. But in terms of popular anticipation, opportunity for attainment of a cabinet post is still considered reasonably fair, especially for the "self-made man" who achieves success in the business world.[3]

From what levels of American society have the ninety-two individuals who served on the Supreme Court been chosen? To answer this question, the membership of the Supreme Court was analyzed in six relatively distinct historical periods. The periods selected were categorized in accordance with the general designation accorded each era by modern historians.[4] One purpose in distinguishing distinct eras was to determine whether the historical patterns of judicial recruitment are in conformity with the predominant social and political trends. The historical periods were (a) 1789–1828, a period in which government was largely by members of the gentry class; (b) 1829–1861, the era of the Jacksonian social and political revolution; (c) 1862–1888, a period in which wealth, particularly corporate, tended to merge with political power; (d) 1889–1919, a period in which corporate influence in government continued to grow, but also an era of rising demands for social justice; (e) 1920–1932, a period of conservative retrenchment and corporate ascendancy in government; and (f) 1933–1959, the era of the Rooseveltian social revolution and its aftermath.

Among the diverse criteria available for the establishment of social status, paternal occupations, patterns of occupational heredity, individual career patterns, ethnic origin, religion, and education have been considered most useful by social scientists.[5] Of these, paternal occupation has been accepted as the most trustworthy clue to the determination of social origin.[6] The great amount of work in judicial biography completed in the last three decades has resulted in the accumulation in readily available form of much of the material necessary for such a synthesis.

Paternal Occupations

Throughout the entire history of the Supreme Court, only a handful of its members were of essentially humble origin. Nine persons selected in widely scattered historical periods comprise the total. The remaining 83 (91 per cent) not only were from families in comfortable economic circumstances but were chosen overwhelmingly from the socially prestigeful and politically influential gentry class in the late eighteenth and early nineteenth century or the professionalized upper-middle class thereafter. A large number of justices (55, comprising 60 per cent of the total) came from politically active families. The politically active families were essentially those enjoying high social status (99 per cent of the political activity was concentrated in families of high social status).

The relation of the patterns of judicial selection to the tendencies frequently attributed to each historical period was generally close but not identical. During 1789–1828, with only one exception, justices were drawn from families rather clearly identified with the gentry class in their states or localities. In the period of Jacksonian Democracy, 1829–1861, three of a total of fourteen justices were chosen from families engaged in occupations of low social status. One might conclude that the Supreme Court was but lightly affected by the democratization of social and political relations which took place in this era.[7] Conversely, the tendencies shown in the succeeding two periods, 1862–1888 and 1889–1919, were quite consistent with the general historical descriptions of the era of corporate ascendancy—in family background the justices almost invariably were drawn from the "better" classes of society. A further decline in the influence of politically prominent families also took place in the first of these two periods. An increasing number of justices were drawn from families which did not have a heritage of political activity but enjoyed prominence in professional or otherwise economically advantaged social circles. However, after 1889, the percentage of justices chosen from politically active families began again to rise—60 per cent (1889–1919) and 72 per cent (1920–1932). By the period 1920–1932, the pattern of economic representation was changed by the appointment of one man of humble origin, Pierce Butler. The final period, 1933–1959, was similar to the Jacksonian period in that three members of the Court were chosen from families of humble origin. It differed, however, in that the gradual decline in the number of families engaged in political activity, which had occurred in the age of

Jackson, became an exceedingly sharp decline to the lowest percentage in the Court's history, 31 per cent.

After 1862, a definite shift in the occupational emphasis of high
social status families took place. The trend began in the Jacksonian
period, but before the 1860's the preponderance of high social
status families had been engaged in nonprofessional occupations
such as farming or manufacturing. A rather high percentage of
the heads of these families had pursued active and successful
political careers. After 1862, the majority of fathers of justices
selected from high social status backgrounds were engaged in
professional activities, largely in the fields of law, medicine,
and religion, and occasionally in higher education. In social com-
position, the over-all tendency was a gradual transition from selection largely from the families of the aristocratic landholding and
mercantile class of the late eighteenth and early nineteenth century
to choice from among members of the professionalized upper-
middle class. Lest this transition from selection from the old
gentry class to predominant influence by the upper-middle class
be interpreted as a liberalizing trend, it might be noted that the
appointees from professionalized upper-middle class families were
firmly in the ascendancy from 1889 through 1937, a period in
which the Court virtually surpassed John Marshall's Court in its
decisions in support of economic conservatism.

Occupational "Heredity"

The social transmission of attitudes, beliefs, values, and
aspirations has as its most effective vehicle the family. Since
political participation of a very advanced kind appears as a crucial
ingredient in the life careers of all but one of the members of
the Supreme Court, the nature and extent of family conditioning for such participation deserves special attention.

The United States has never produced an aristocracy comparable to Namier's "inevitable Parliament men," [8] but it has
developed, especially in local and state politics, families with
consistent and frequently successful records of political involvement. America's "political families" have been able to transmit

intangible, yet real advantages to their children. These advantages have included not only the prestige of possession of a "political" name and family connections in a local, state, or even national political organization,[9] but also a true political education which is derived from the practice and familiarity with political activity, the encouragement of political ambitions, expectations, and perhaps a veritable sense of destiny respecting high political achievement.

Nearly two thirds of the members of the Supreme Court were raised in this far from commonplace type of American family. Such a fact is not especially surprising in the earliest period of court selection, 1789–1828, because of the proclivity of the members of the gentry class for assumption of political responsibility and leadership. But the high incidence of political family names found in the roster of the Supreme Court after 1829 would indicate that the values and aspirations of these families were those of what has often been referred to as the "old" rather than the "new" upper-middle class.[10] It should not be assumed that the knowledge of the political attachments of these families would provide a neat index of the judicial predilections of their sons who attained positions on the Supreme Court. Rather, such background probably contributed a high sense of political expectation and a political style which denoted familiarity with the political realities.

These factors were probably of crucial importance for the justices who were drawn from families with a firm tradition of judicial service. To an even greater extent than the function of over-all political participation, that of judicial service is exceedingly rare in America. Yet twelve justices were the sons of prominent judges (usually of the highest court of a state).[11] Six (including one of the above) married the daughters of judges.[12] An additional fifteen were related to prominent jurists.[13] Excluding duplication, thirty-two members of the Supreme Court (over one third) were related to jurists and intimately connected with families possessing a tradition of judicial service.

Several of these families have had members or close relations on the Supreme Court for periods extending over a half-century. For example, Sarah Williamson of Georgia was the grandmother of Justice John Archibald Campbell (who served on the Court from 1853–1861) and the great-grandmother of Justice Lucius Q. C. Lamar (1888–1893). Later Joseph Ruckner Lamar, a cousin of Lucius, also served on the Court from 1910– 1916. The Livingston family of New York and New Jersey has also had an intimate relation to Supreme Court service through many generations. John Jay, the first Chief Justice (1789– 1795), was married to a Livingston whose father was a prominent colonial judge. Jay's wife's brother, Brockholst Livingston, served on the Court from 1806 to 1823. And Brockholst was succeeded on the Supreme Court by Smith Thompson, who had married into the Livingston family. Thompson served on the highest court from 1823 to 1843.

Sorokin, in his pioneering work on *Social Mobility*, observed that the incidence of occupational heredity in the United States had decreased in the early part of the twentieth century but that the trend had not been universal. Of American society he concluded that "inheritance of wealth, the social position of a family, its traditions, its reputation, all continue to play— juridically and psychologically—a very considerable part, even in a democratic society, in establishing an individual's reputation." [14]

This concluding observation has especial relevance to the selection of members of the Supreme Court, for as was observed above, nearly two thirds were drawn from politically active families; of perhaps greater significance, a third of this group were chosen from a relatively narrow circle of families—families which have been distinctive in their possession of traditions of judicial service. This fact does not imply that a deliberate effort has been made by successive Presidents to choose Supreme Court justices from such families; rather, that it frequently was very advantageous for a successful lawyer and a member of the President's political party to be a member of a family with a political background, and especially with a strong tradition of judicial service. This situation was as true in 1955 for John Marshall Harlan, the namesake and grandson of the famed dissenter in *Plessy* v.

Ferguson, as it was in 1799 for Alfred Moore, the son of a well-known colonial judge of North Carolina, or in 1874 for Morrison R. Waite, the son of a former Chief Justice of the Supreme Court of Connecticut.

Where Were the Justices Born?

Closely related to the question of the determination of social origins and the nature of the relation of family background to social outlook is the additional environmental factor of place of birth and the setting for the formative years of the justices. Even in the earliest period, a greater number of the justices (75 per cent) were born (and usually reared) in cities or towns. Because most of the families of the justices possessed unusual social and economic advantages, the justices who were born in an urban environment were not subject to the tensions and crowded conditions of the tenement areas and slums. For many, the fact that they lived in a city brought all the urban cultural advantages but maintained the serenity and security also enjoyed by the justices living on plantations and town or country estates.

In a few instances, place of birth also had a special relation to United States citizenship. An overwhelming number (94.6 per cent) of the justices were, of course, born in the United States of parents who were citizens of the United States. Six justices were born abroad, Justice David Brewer in Turkey of American missionaries. Three of the foreign-born justices were chosen for the Supreme Court by President Washington: James Iredell (England), James Wilson (Scotland), and William Paterson (Ireland). The remaining two, George Sutherland (England) and Felix Frankfurter (Austria), were chosen in modern times. Leaving aside Washington's appointees, both Sutherland and Frankfurter came to America at an early age. Their childhood experiences were similar to those of first-generation Americans rather than aliens. Although nativists raised objections to Frankfurter's appointment, other factors were present to assure presidential nomination and to assure senatorial confirmation.

On the basis of these selection patterns, it would seem apparent that the foreign-born ordinarily have only remote possibilities for attainment of a seat on the Supreme Court. In a roughly comparable period, 374 of 9,618 Congressmen were foreign-born.[15] Yet, on a percentage basis, opportunity for attainment of a Supreme Court appointment has been greater than that for election to Congress, since 5.5 per cent of the total Court membership was foreign-born, while only 2.6 per cent of the members of Congress were in this category. Generally speaking, of course, the members of the Supreme Court have been chosen from among American families that have been long established in the New World. These families, it might be added, often exhibited the firm social and political leadership in the community which has as one of its foundations an early American heritage.

Ethnic Origins of the Justices

The ethnic origins of members of the Supreme Court represent another important source of data available for the determination of their social background.[16] Throughout the entire history of the Supreme Court, judicial recruitment has granted a virtual monopoly to natives or the descendants of natives of northwestern Europe. And among those selected, individuals of English, Welsh, Scotch, or Irish ethnic origin have predominated, comprising 88 per cent of the appointees. No person of African or Asiatic ethnic origin has been appointed to the Court, nor has such a person even been nominated. The justices originating ethnically in northwestern Europe, but outside the British Isles, totaled seven, including four of French derivation (John Jay, Gabriel Duval, Lucius Q. C. Lamar, and Joseph R. Lamar), two of Dutch derivation (William Johnson and Willis Van Devanter), and one of Norwegian ethnic stock (Earl Warren). Those of central, eastern, or southern European derivation comprise a tiny group of five justices, four of whom were of Germanic (including Austrian and German-Bohemian) derivation (John Catron, Samuel F. Miller, Louis Brandeis, and Felix Frankfurter), while one justice was of Iberian derivation (Benjamin N. Cardozo). Among the large ethnic groupings of European origin which have never been represented on the Supreme Court are the Italians and Southern and Eastern Slavs.

The Supreme Court is, of course, not a representative institution, but the pattern of judicial selection has tacitly recognized the coming of age politically of many, but not all, of the ethnic and religious groups in America. Discussion of the ethnic factor is virtually absent from the available presidential evaluations of potential nominees,[17] but it is very likely that individuals belonging to ethnic groups which are unpopular would not be considered potential candidates in the first place. Furthermore, instances where criticism of the "race" of a nominee (such as of Hoover's selection of Cardozo) have been recorded usually were basically directed against the nominee's religion. Only during the earliest period, 1789–1828, has the ethnic variation in the Supreme Court's membership been a rough approximation of the ethnic divisions within the total American population. In subsequent periods, as the proportion of ethnic groups of non-British origin grew,[18] the disparities in ethnic representation on the Supreme Court became greater.

The patterns of ethnic representation are additional evidences of the virtual monopolization of Supreme Court appointments by the socially privileged segment of the population dubbed the "old Americans." [19]

Religious Affiliation of the Justices

Religious diversity in America has at its root a social basis as well as a doctrinal rationale. To some denominations are attached factors of prestige and social status, while others are viewed socially as "churches of the disinherited," of unpopular immigrant groups, or of ethnic groups which, because of color, have not been fully accepted.[20] In keeping with the fact that most of the justices were selected from among socially advantaged families was the heavy incidence of affiliation with high social status religious groups by the justices. An overwhelming majority were Protestant. A substantial majority of the justices were affiliated with the Episcopalian, Presbyterian (or French Calvinist), Congregational, and Unitarian churches. Slightly over 10 per cent were affiliated with Protestant religious groups which historically were considered of lower social status. In a special category were the slightly less than 10 per cent of the justices who were either Roman Catholic, Jewish, or Quaker. Only one Quaker, Noah Swayne, has been appointed to the Supreme Court. Since the Roman Catholic and Jewish groups in America have frequently been subjected to nativist and religious criticism and attack,[21] members of these groups have, historically, been at a considerable disadvantage in the competition for Supreme Court appointments.

In recent years there has been considerable discussion of the existence of a custom of maintaining on the Supreme Court a member of the Roman Catholic and Jewish religious faiths. Has such a custom been recognized by appointing Presidents and if so, how did it become established?

In terms of Roman Catholic court members, the appointment of Chief Justice Roger Brooke Taney cannot be accounted the conscious beginning of the tradition of Catholic appointments, because the religious aspect of his selection was obviously a very minor consideration for President Jackson. Clearly, Taney's ideological soundness and political services plus Jackson's desire to vindicate an earlier senatorial rejection of Taney as an associate justice were of far greater importance. Not until the second term of President Cleveland was a second Roman Catholic appointed: Edward D. White. Here again it is not at all clear that religion was of importance. Although the religious factor was not ignored, White's party consistency, the fact that Cleveland could, at one stroke, rid himself of a strong senatorial opponent of his tariff program (who was otherwise ideologically sound) and force a recalcitrant Senate to confirm his nominee, plus White's personal friendship with Cleveland, all played more decisive roles in the appointment process. Similarly, there is little evidence to show that Joseph McKenna was appointed to establish or maintain a tradition of Catholic representation on the Supreme Court. For one thing, White was still on the Court at the time of McKenna's appointment, the two serving together for several years. Mc-

Kenna's appointment has been attributed chiefly to his Republican orthodoxy and political services, the influence of California railroad magnate Leland Stanford, and his close friendship and associations with William McKinley, who as President appointed him.

Similarly, the appointment of Pierce Butler by President Harding could not be termed a recognition of a custom of religious representation, because McKenna was still on the Court at the time of Butler's choice. President Warren Harding was under considerable Catholic pressure, but it should be recognized that the appointment of a nominal Democrat who was a known economic conservative and a highly successful corporation lawyer was considered smart politically and safe ideologically. As in most situations, it is not clear which of these factors was decisive in Harding's choice,[22] but the religious factor could scarcely be deemed an overriding consideration.

President Roosevelt's choice of Frank Murphy was probably a clear-cut example of the recognition of a need to give Roman Catholics representation on the Court but did not involve the crossing of party lines. Murphy was not only a Democrat but had been active politically and was recognized as an ideologically sound New Dealer. When Murphy died, however, President Truman replaced him with a non-Catholic. Consequently, for the first time since the second administration of Grover Cleveland, the Roman Catholic segment of the population was unrepresented on the Supreme Court.

President Eisenhower's selection of William Brennan, a Catholic, a New Jersey Democrat, and a state judge, again provided the Roman Catholic religious group representation on the Supreme Court, but it also fulfilled several other functions. Because the appointment was made just before the presidential election of 1956, some observers noted that it provided President Eisenhower an opportunity to demonstrate his peculiar ability for remaining "above politics" while at the same time taking an action which might have considerable appeal among normally Democratic urban eastern Catholics. The choice of Brennan, generally evaluated as an able state judge, was also consistent with Eisenhower's stated objective of choosing appointees who had prior judicial experience.

Like the Roman Catholic appointments, Jewish representation on the Supreme Court was not consciously initiated but became established after the initial appointment of an individual belonging to that religious group. Although the first such appointment did not occur until the presidency of Woodrow Wilson, as early as 1853, Whig President Millard Fillmore offered a Supreme Court appointment to Senator-elect Judah Benjamin of Louisiana. Benjamin preferred to take his seat in the United States Senate and, as a consequence, his name was not submitted.[23] President Woodrow Wilson's nomination of Louis Brandeis was based overwhelmingly upon ideological rather than religious grounds. Wilson's strong desire in this repect is sadly summed up in his letter to Justice John Hessin Clarke concerning the latter's resignation on September 18, 1922. Wrote Wilson, "Like thousands of other liberals throughout the country, I have been counting on the influence of you and Justice Brandeis to restrain the Court in some measure from the extreme reactionary course which it seems inclined to follow. . . ."[24]

The second appointment of an individual of the Jewish faith was that of Benjamin Cardozo. Since Justice Brandeis was still serving on the Court, Cardozo's appointment in no sense could be termed a perpetuation of a custom of religious representation. Since President Hoover made this choice in a manner which ignored all the "rules" customarily governing such choices, it might be validly assumed that merit was the only consideration. Hoover had to violate the conception of geographical representation; Cardozo became the third New Yorker on the Court. Furthermore, Hoover disregarded not only the rule of party (for Cardozo was a Democrat) but also the ideological rule (for Cardozo was a known liberal). McHargue points out that the letters from prominent civic, bar, religious, labor, business, and educational leaders to President Hoover in Cardozo's behalf represented the most impressive intervention of this kind on record.[25] Cardozo had established an outstanding reputation as a state jurist and writer in legal philosophy, and was considered by intellectual leaders and the leaders of the bar as the logical successor to the justice who had resigned, Oliver Wendell Holmes. Ultimately, President Hoover justifiably received credit for an exceptionally courageous and outstanding appointment.

So far as the clear recognition of a need for Jewish representation is concerned, it was probably not fully recognized until President Franklin Roosevelt chose Professor Felix Frankfurter of the Harvard Law School as Justice Cardozo's successor. Here again, however, it is not at all clear that the religious factor was of primary importance. Frankfurter was considered politically and ideologically sound and was recognized as an eminent legal scholar. Like several of Roosevelt's later appointees, Frankfurter was not a practicing lawyer but an academician. As such he was considered more desirable by Roosevelt because of his broader social, economic, and philosophical outlook than the more narrowly-oriented legal practitioners.

In each of the modern situations which have been publicly acclaimed as perpetuations of a "custom" of religious representation—the appointments of Felix Frankfurter, Frank Murphy, and William Brennan—most of the other "rules" of judicial selection have been observed. It may be implied that the selections by Republican Presidents of Roman Catholic Democrats were, in part, attempts at weakening the traditional Roman Catholic allegiance to the Democratic party. Alone among modern presidents, Harry Truman openly refused to recognize the existence of the tradition. When asked, after the death of Justice Murphy, whether the Supreme Court "should have at least one representative of each major minority religious community," President Truman had replied that he "did not believe religions had anything to do with the Supreme Bench. If an individual has the qualifications," Mr. Truman added, "he did not care if he is a Protestant, Catholic, or Jew." [26] From President Truman's experience in denying the necessity for considering religions in the appointment process a lesson may be drawn. The very controversy over the existence of the "custom" has political significance, and it may be assumed that the religious representation, whether accepted or not, must play a part in subsequent presidential considerations of judicial selections.

Educational Background of the Justices

Of all the advantages which were incidental to birth into the early gentry class or the professionalized upper-middle class, that of the opportunity to acquire a good education was perhaps of greatest importance to the later formative period in the career patterns of a majority of the justices. A college education has, until comparatively recent times, been a prize available only to a small minority of American adults. An advanced education in a college or university of high standing has been even more rare. And finally, such an education coupled with professional training in law has been exceedingly difficult to attain. A rather large number of justices have been able to acquire such education, usually in the better colleges and universities. Over a third did their college work in the Ivy League schools, while nearly a third did their law studies in them. Aside from the manifest professional advantages which might be derived from such educational opportunities, the personal associations which were established and the notions of social responsibility and civic leadership inculcated at these educational institutions must all be taken into account as aids in the individual career patterns of the justices and as factors conditioning their attitudes toward the challenges and responsibilities of judicial decision making in later maturity.

The justices who studied under private tutors and who served law apprenticeships were not recipients of inferior types of education. In fact, these justices were often afforded several unique advantages from this educational opportunity, for in most instances the tutors or law teachers not only were unusually talented but were leading practitioners of law in the community or state, and were among the top political leaders in the contemporary scene. One may conclude that in the period before the full development of law schools, members of the Supreme Court who were taught law by outstanding legal and political leaders gained incalculable educational and political advantages in the process. Throughout the history of the Supreme Court, the recruitment process has generally rewarded those whose educational backgrounds, both legal and nonlegal, have comprised the rare combination of intellectual, social, and political opportunities which have generally been available only to the economically comfortable and socially prominent segment of the American population.

The Nonpolitical Occupations of the Court Members

Of all the customs, real or fancied, which purportedly govern the selection of appointees to the Supreme Court, that of choosing men engaged in the legal profession has been adhered to most rigidly. For all intents and purposes, the federal Constitution would more accurately reflect American judicial recruitment practices by requiring that the selection process be limited to individuals who are lawyers. All of the ninety-two justices of the Supreme Court had legal training of some kind. All practiced law at some stage in their careers. For eighty-eight of the total (97 per cent), law was a major nonpolitical occupation. The justices who had not practiced law as a major nonpolitical occupation (Stone, Frankfurter, Douglas, and Rutledge) were all law school professors or deans. With the exception of Stone, all were chosen by President Franklin Roosevelt and were, in essence, instruments of constitutional protest against the highly restrictive attitude of earlier appointees. Roosevelt's penchant for appointing university professors was at one time regarded as a precedent which, once established, would bring into the Supreme Court men with broader sociological, economic, and philosophical training and outlooks than professional and, frequently corporation lawyers have.[27] Roosevelt's appointing policy has, however, not been followed either by President Truman or President Eisenhower.

To indicate simply that most Supreme Court appointees were lawyers tells little about the characteristics of the Court in various historical periods. It is important therefore to know what kind of lawyers they were before appointment to the high Court. In order to do this, the court members were categorized as (a) lawyers who were primarily politicians, (b) lawyers who spent much of their careers in state or federal judicial posts, (c) lawyers who, at the peak of their legal careers, dealt largely as agents of large corporations, (d) lawyers whose practices were largely noncorporate, and (e) lawyers by education who were engaged in primarily academic pursuits.

The fact that an overwhelming number of Supreme Court appointees selected in the first two historical periods (1789–1828 and 1828–1861) pursued primarily political careers should scarcely occasion surprise. The pattern for frankly partisan appointment was set by George Washington himself and re-emphasized by John Adams and Thomas Jefferson for their respective political parties.

After 1862 a substantial, but not large, number of corporation lawyers were appointed to the Supreme Court, constituting 19 per cent in 1862–1888, 22 per cent in 1889–1919, 29 per cent in 1920–1932, and then declining to 14 per cent in 1933–1959. Although all except the last of these periods corresponded with historical eras in which corporate influence was, with brief contrary interludes, ascendant in the national government, it would appear at first glance that the process of appointing members of the Supreme Court had remained relatively immune from such influence. This was not true, however, because ideological soundness, from the corporate point of view, actually found its most reliable advocates among the appointees with extensive judicial careers.

The number of appointees who had pursued primarily political careers took a sharp decline after 1862, dropping from 63 per cent in the Jacksonian era to 32 per cent in 1862–1888, 33 per cent in 1889–1919, and 29 per cent in 1920–1932. In the final period, 1933–1959, political careerists on the Court rose to 62 per cent. None of these periods rivaled the original one, 1789–1828, in which 85 per cent of the Court appointees were lawyers who had pursued primarily political careers. It should be noted, however, that with only one exception, George Shiras, every member of the Supreme Court had actively participated in politics before his appointment to the nation's highest tribunal.

In actuality the most important change in the pattern of judicial selection which occurred after 1862 was the great increase in the percentage of men chosen who had primarily judicial careers. For two periods, judges from state courts or inferior federal courts constituted the largest single group of appointees, totaling 45 per cent in 1862–1888 and 1889–1919, declining to 29 per cent in 1920–1932 and then dropping sharply to a mere 6 per cent in the final period, 1933–1959. Not all the members of the Supreme Court who had prior judicial experience were included in this group. It was felt to be more realistic to include only those whose prior judicial experience represented a major portion of their adult careers. For example, from among the Eisenhower appointees only William Brennan pursued primarily a judicial career. Harlan, Whittaker, and Stewart had short federal judicial tenures before appointment to the Supreme Court, but through most of their adult careers they were corporation lawyers.

The very fact that all the members of the Supreme Court were members of the legal profession in itself merits consideration as a conditioner of social, economic, and political attitudes. Whether one accepts the belief of Alexis de Tocqueville that "the seat of the American aristocracy is with the judges on the bench and the lawyers at the bar" or the contradictory view of a contemporary critic that "the members of the legal profession . . . are not the aristocracy but the agents of the aristocracy . . . [which] is constituted by the owners of accumulated wealth," [28] there has been rather general agreement that the influence of the bar in America has been essentially conservative.[29] This does not imply that every lawyer appointed to the Supreme Court has succumbed to this conservative influence, but it is clear that all are exposed to it. There is considerable evidence to indicate that many lawyers on the high bench willingly espoused the sort of legal conservatism exemplified in the leadership and ideology of the American Bar Association. Furthermore, a number of the members of the Court, such as William Howard

Taft and George Sutherland, were among the leaders of the bar, both before and after their appointments to the Supreme Court, who developed and cherished its conservative traditions and attitudes.

Political Party and Ideological Constancy

The mere recitation of the changing patterns of legal careers represented on the Supreme Court lacks meaningfulness except as a descriptive contribution. When considered in connection with the most important of the customary "rules" of the judicial selection process, however, these patterns assume greater significance. The choice of men ideologically committed or thought to be committed to the values of the President making the selection has been the policy most rigidly adhered to throughout American history.[30]

One clue to the explanation for the pre-Civil War tendency toward choice of lawyers who pursued primarily political careers lay in the fact that during much of this period party affiliation generally included acceptance of certain clearly defined social, economic, and constitutional attitudes. One need consider only the following statement of Thomas Jefferson to recognize the clarity with which early party leaders identified party loyalty and "right thinking" on philosophical, social, and economic ideas. Jefferson, writing to President Madison's Postmaster, Gideon Granger, suggested that the old Federalist justice William Cushing be replaced with "a firm unequivocal republican, whose principles are born with him, and not an occasion ingraftment, as necessary to complete the great reformation in our government to which the nation gave its fiat ten years ago." [31] Even in the pre-Civil War era, this identity of party and values was not always present, as the appointment of Joseph Story so amply demonstrated, but after 1862, the relation between party affiliation and ideological commitment became, if anything, increasingly less clear.[32]

The judicial selection process reveals rather convincingly that the selection of individuals of the President's political affiliation served not only as a method of rewarding political supporters but also as one of several means of identification of a judicial candidate's ideology, although there has usually been strong pressure for both party and ideological consistency. To be sure, presidents have occasionally paid off political debts (as may have been true in the appointment of Justice Catron), [33] or perhaps have "kicked upstairs" bothersome cabinet officers (as has been alleged in the selection of Justice McLean), [34] but the so-called crasser political motives have not generally been determinative in the appointment of members of the Supreme Court. During historical periods when party attachment actually meant commitment to certain recognizable social, economic, or philosophical values, the choice of justices rather consistently followed party lines. When the identity of party label and ideology was uncertain, presidents usually exercised greater care in their assessment of ideological consistency.

Among the biographical materials on presidents, the frank correspondence between Theodore Roosevelt and Senator Henry Cabot Lodge concerning Oliver Wendell Holmes in 1902 and Horace Lurton in 1906 remains a classic illustration of the realities of Supreme Court selection. Of the possibility of selecting Judge Oliver Wendell Holmes, a Republican, and a member of the Supreme Judicial Court of Massachusetts, President Roosevelt obviously felt that a mere party label was not sufficiently indicative of Holmes' basic values and, consequently, required more information. To Lodge he wrote,

> I should like to know that Judge Holmes was in entire sympathy with our views, that is, with your views and mine . . . before I would feel justified in appointing him . . . . I should hold myself guilty of an irreparable wrong to the nation if I should put . . . [upon the Court] any man who was not absolutely sane and sound on the great national policies for which we stand in public life.[35]

President Roosevelt's letter to Lodge concerning Horace Lurton, a Democrat, and a federal judge, is even more precise with reference to the ideological prerequisities of his appointees. Wrote Roosevelt,

> Nothing has been so strongly born in on me concerning lawyers on the bench as that the nominal politics of the man has nothing to do with his actions on the bench. His *real* politics are all-important. In Lurton's case, Taft and Day, his two former associates, are very desirous of having him on. He is right on the Negro question; he is right on the power of the federal government; he is right on the Insular business; he is right about corporations, he is right about labor. On every question that would come before the bench, he has so far shown himself to be in much closer touch with the policies in which you and I believe than even White because he has been right about corporations where White has been wrong.[36]

It is rather important to note that Democrat Horace Lurton, despite his ideological soundness, *did not* get this appointment. (Lurton was, however, later chosen for the Supreme Court by Theodore Roosevelt's successor, William Howard Taft.) Instead, Roosevelt appointed his Republican Attorney General, William Henry Moody. In all probability, Senator Lodge's reply to the letter quoted above contains both the explanation for Roosevelt's failure to appoint Lurton and further insight regarding the traditional balancing of factors in the judicial selection process. Lodge wrote,

> I am glad that Lurton holds all the opinions that you say he does and that you are so familiar with his views. I need hardly say that those are the very questions on which I am just as anxious as you that judges should hold what we consider sound opinions, *but I do not see why Republicans cannot be found who hold those opinions as well as Democrats.* . . .
>   Of course you know my high opinion of Moody. . . . Nothing would give me greater pleasure than to see him on the bench.[37]

Lodge's successful intervention on behalf of Moody suggests that the presidential role in the judicial selection process might occasionally be overemphasized. It is certain that while presidents have usually dominated the selection process by determining the ideological prerequisites of their nominees, the role of the Senate cannot be overlooked. Particularly in periods in which a president lacked party or ideological support in the Senate, the influence of senatorial confirmation assumed far-reaching importance. Approximately one fifth of the presidential nominations for Supreme Court appointments have been dealt with negatively by the Senate, either by outright rejection, failure to act, or postponement.[38] Since the administration of Grover Cleveland, only one presidential nominee, Judge Parker, has been rejected, but the Senate frequently scrutinizes the candidates closely.

The Senate has occasionally turned down nominees because they were clearly poor selections (such as Madison's choice of the Connecticut political manager Alexander Wolcott, and Grant's choice of the corrupt George Williams). However, its record with regard to consideration of the merits of presidential nominees is spotty, for only Roscoe Conkling's own declination of a Supreme Court seat after senatorial confirmation saved the nation from the appointment of the great spoilsman. The primary considerations in senatorial disapproval of presidential nominations have been party and ideology. The rejection of President Andrew Jackson's nomination of Roger Brooke Taney for an associate justiceship in 1835 [39] is an excellent illustration. The Senate was dominated by an anti-Jackson coalition led by Henry Clay, Daniel Webster, and John C. Calhoun. This coalition, which had the backing of Nicholas Biddle and the supporters of the United States Bank, was particularly opposed to Taney because of his record as Secretary of the Treasury. The measure of ideological scrutiny given this nominee by the dominant coalition in the Senate is well summed up in the following excerpt from a conservative newspaper:

> We hope that the Senate will not only apply the veto to the pretensions of this man, but that it will pass a decided resolution to oppose the elevation of any man *who is not perfectly sound in regard to the fundamental principles of the Constitution as expounded by Daniel Webster.*[40]

It is interesting to note that presidents and their Senates have always had nominees whose political bona fides were matters of wide knowledge. Every member of the Supreme Court except George Shiras held a political post of some kind prior to his appointment to the high bench.[41] Several of the justices had also been unsuccessful candidates for political offices which were of greater importance than those which they actually attained prior to their appointment to the Supreme Court.

Since state or federal judicial service is included among the political posts categorized, special consideration should be given to the factor of prior judicial experience.

The Prior Judicial Experience of Members of the Supreme Court

In recent years a great deal of attention has been focused upon the question whether individuals should have judicial experience before they are considered eligible for appointment to the Supreme Court of the United States. President Eisenhower, after his appointment of Earl Warren, imposed such a standard, choosing Harlan, Brennan, Whittaker, and Stewart from the federal or state benches.[42] On April 30, 1956, Senator Smathers proposed that Congress formalize this policy by adopting a statutory requirement that all future appointees to the Supreme Court have at least five years judicial experience either in an inferior federal court or in the highest court of a state.[43] It may be assumed that the similarity of objectives does not reflect a similarity of motives. The ostensible justifications for these proposals were identical, however. Both the President and the congressional supporters of prior judicial experience argued that individuals possessing such experience are more likely to develop attitudes of restraint which, at least by implication are alleged to be lacking in "political" appointees. For Southern Congressmen, the matter is put somewhat differently. With the shadow of *Brown* v. *Board of Education* cast over them, they bitterly urge the selection of men who will base decisions, according to this argument, upon "law," not "sociology." It may be properly suspected that those who urge this method of selection assume, consciously or subconsciously, that "good" judges are those who are apt to render decisions in accordance with the ideological predilections of the sponsors of this change in method of judicial selection.

The contemporary advocacy of prior judicial experience as a prerequisite for Supreme Court appointment is only the most recent of the manifestations of the fact that advocacy of particular methods of judicial selection is inexorably related to desires for ideological control of the Court. This truth may be made more apparent by an analysis of the type of men on the Supreme Court who have had prior judicial experience. Well over 50 per cent of the justices had served in a judicial capacity at some time before appointment to the Supreme Court, but only slightly more than 25 per cent had had really extensive judicial careers. It is upon this latter group of justices whose life careers prior to appointment to the Supreme Court had been primarily judicial that attention will be centered.[44]

The considerations which governed the choice of these judicially trained men varied according to changing circumstances. During the period of Jeffersonian and Jacksonian dominance of the national administration, Supreme Court appointments were often viewed with an eye to the local responsibilities of the justices while on circuit duty. Thus acquaintance with the peculiarities of the land laws of the states within a circuit was occasionally considered a prerequisite, as, for example, in the choices of Thomas Todd and Robert Trimble. Particularly before 1891, experience in the "federal specialities," such as admiralty law, was also of importance.[45] However, it is not at all clear that experience on an inferior federal court or a state court is necessary to or intimately related to the sort of service performed on the nation's highest court. As Justice Frankfurter has ably put it,

> The Supreme Court is a very special kind of court. "Judicial service" as such has no significant relation to the kinds of litigation that come before the Supreme Court, to the types of issues they raise, to qualities that these actualities require for wise decision.[46]

Frankfurter clearly recognized that it might be argued that even "if experience on a state [or inferior federal] court does not adequately prepare even the greatest of judges for the problems . . . of the Supreme Court, judicial experience intrinsically fosters certain habits of mind and attitudes . . . which are indeed preconditions for the wise exercise of the judicial function of the Supreme Court." Justice Frankfurter himself dealt with this by stating that fewer justices without prior judicial experience "dallied with political ambition" than those who possessed such experience.[47] However, the problem of political ambition, whether directed toward the Presidency or, as is frequently overlooked, toward promotion to the Chief Justiceship, represents only one facet of a broader ideological problem. To put it bluntly, there is little evidence to support the view that individuals with primarily judicial careers before selection to the Supreme Court were more objective than those without such experience. And this statement is generally true whether or not they cherished political ambitions.

There are several historical factors which support this conclusion. First, appointment to an inferior federal judgeship has generally been in the nature of a political reward for recognized partisans.[48] The process of selection of inferior federal judges, which has always been essentially based on patronage, is hardly conducive to the choice of judges who are apt to be aloof to party or ideological issues. Secondly, the choice of prominent state judges similarly draws upon men who usually have had to make strong party and ideological commitments in order to achieve high judicial office in their states. This situation has been less true in some states than in others, but, generally speaking, high state judicial office has required party and ideological commitments whether the posts be appointive or elective. Furthermore, the biographies of many of the prominent state judges who achieved a position on the nation's highest court bear this out. Men like Justices Catron or Davis, despite the fact that they served in state judicial posts for much of their adult careers, were primary political managers.

Finally, the men chosen for the Supreme Court from the inferior federal bench or higher state courts have almost uniformly been strong ideological partisans. Justice David Brewer's often quoted declaration that the paternalistic system of government is odious, is illustrative of the kind of partisanship which was part of the make-up of most of the justices who had extensive judicial experience before their Supreme Court appointment. The penchant for presidents to appoint such men, especially during the periods 1862–1888 and 1889–1919 (when such appointees comprised 45 per cent of the Supreme Court), reflected, not a desire to choose men who were aloof, but rather a purposeful determination to select known ideological partisans. When they were inferior federal judges or state judges, men like Field, Brewer, Strong, Brown, Howell Jackson, Pitney, or Lurton made their reputations as individuals who were apt to take a conservative view on government regulation of private enterprise and, sometimes, as stern judicial administrators in their treatment of labor unions. For presidents looking for Supreme Court appointees with these qualities, service on the inferior federal bench or higher state courts provided a readily available index to the assessment of the personal and intellectual qualities of potential candidates. Similarly, such prior judicial experience provided the sort of knowledge of individual career patterns desired by interest groups [49] which have, particularly since the Civil War, sought to influence appointments to the Supreme Court.

There is little in the history of the Supreme Court to suggest that justices with prior judicial experience were more objective or better qualified than those who lacked such experience. As a matter of fact, despite the examples of Holmes and Cardozo, some of the Supreme Court's most distinguished members, notably Marshall, Taney, Curtis, Campbell, Miller, Bradley, Hughes, Brandeis,[50] and Stone, were totally lacking in this experience before their appointments to the Supreme Court.

The Significance of Social and
Political Background Factors

The presidential choice of a member of the Supreme Court has always been an object of great public attention contemporaneously and a subject of keen interest to public law commentators and historians after the event. Most treatments have centered attention upon the reasons, ostensible or real, for the individual selections made by a particular president. It is important, however, to consider the collective aspects of the judicial selection process in order, first, to establish the pattern of recruitment, and secondly, to examine in tentative fashion some of the possible relations between social and political background factors and decision making tendencies.

Throughout American history there has been an overwhelming tendency for presidents to choose nominees for the Supreme Court from among the socially advantaged families. The typical Supreme Court justice has invariably been white, generally Protestant with a penchant for a high social status denomination, usually of ethnic stock originating in the British Isles, and born in comfortable circumstances in an urban or small town environment. In the earlier history of the Court, he very likely was born in the aristocratic gentry class, although later he tended to come from the professionalized upper-middle class. Whereas nearly two thirds of his fellows were selected from politically active families, a third of his fellows were chosen from families having a tradition of judicial service. In college and legal education, the average justice was afforded opportunities for training and associations which were most advantageous. It seems reasonable to assume that very few sons of families outside the upper, or upper-middle, social and economic classes have been able to acquire the particular type of education and the subsequent professional, and especially political, associations which appear to be unwritten prerequisites for appointment to the nation's highest tribunal.

Educational opportunity emerges as a crucial ingredient in judicial recruitment. Every member of the Supreme Court was the recipient of law training and a great number were afforded college or university educations prior to their law training. Law training not only fulfilled an unwritten educational requirement for judicial appointment but frequently represented an important stage in the development of individual political careers. Especially during the periods before the widespread acceptance of law schools as the primary centers for legal education, the internship of subsequent members of the Supreme Court in the law offices of prominent practitioners afforded the student not only a unique educational opportunity and valuable professional associations, but frequently the political sponsorship of men who held high office or were influential in the councils of their political organizations.

The influence of family background, while less tangible in certain respects, may be considered of great importance. In an economic sense, birth in a family in comfortable circumstances was generally a precondition for the advanced educational opportunities afforded most Supreme Court members. However, it is important to note that the families of the justices generally were not of the type one identifies with the modern middle class, a type which has become increasingly apolitical, interested more in comfort and economic security than in the assumption of social responsibility.[51] On the contrary, a high percentage of the families of the justices demonstrated a very deep sense of social responsibility and political involvement. It would be a gross oversimplification to assume a direct transferal of the particular political attachments of these families to their sons. Yet the biographical data on the justices evidences a considerable conditioning of broad attitudes toward social and political participation.

Although selection to the Supreme Court has not usually involved the patronage considerations ordinarily associated with judicial appointment to the inferior federal courts, it has generally involved basically political considerations. Just as training in law has been a necessary educational step in the achievement of a Supreme Court appointment, so has political activism been a virtual precondition for such an appointment. The degree of political involvement of aspirants to the Supreme Court has, of course, varied considerably. In a large number of instances the justices, prior to their appointments, not only held high political office but were deeply involved in party and campaign management and had close political associations and personal ties with the men who later nominated and appointed them. Thus political activism of a rather intense kind emerges as a necessary stage in career ascent to the Supreme Court.

Political involvement before Supreme Court appointment ordinarily serves as an effective medium for the identification of the political, social, and economic values of prospective Court members by interest groups seeking to assure the ideological soundness of new appointees. For example, the strong intervention by the President of the Chicago and Northwestern Railroad and the Union Pacific Railroad, William B. Ogden, with the Lincoln administration in behalf of Noah Swayne coincided with the rapid growth of corporate influence at all levels of government in the Civil War and post-Civil War eras. The endorsement of Swayne by Ogden marked the beginning of a period of substantial railroad influence in the appointment of Supreme Court justices.[52]

The appointment of men with prior judicial experience, especially those with extensive careers in the inferior federal courts or the state courts, was of great importance in particular historical periods. These appointments frequently served the practical function of identifying ideological partisans, as did selection from the ranks of the openly avowed political activists.

The picture that emerges in the pattern of recruitment of Supreme Court justices is one which emphasizes the intimacy of judicial and political affairs. Since the most important function of the Supreme Court is the settlement of fundamentally political issues through the medium of judicial review, the political background of the justices undoubtedly represents a very necessary and valuable source of experience and training.

It is not at all clear that the social and political background factors in themselves may serve as reliable indicators of precise patterns of judicial behavior. Explanations based entirely upon the causal influence of such factors as family, economic and social status, ethnic background or religious affiliation could scarcely take into account such important considerations as the impact upon individual justices of the traditions of the Supreme Court itself or of the interaction of intelligent and frequently forceful personalities which has been an integral part of the internal procedure of the Court. Complete dependence upon background factors would also ignore the complexity and subtlety of intellect and motivation which is part of the collective picture of the ninety-two individuals who have sat on the high bench.

The difficulty is illustrated by looking at the over-all judicial reputations of the nine justices of humble origin.[53] It might be argued, for example, that the choice of men of humble origin for the Supreme Court could scarcely be considered dangerous to the rights of private property because the group included James Wilson, John McLean, John Catron, Pierce Butler, and James Byrnes. Perhaps one would be tempted to accept the acid comment, made by a contemporary concerning Catron's personal characteristics, as a sociological explanation of the decision-making predilections of these justices. Catron was described as "profoundly aristocratic in all his habits and bearing *as all men raised to wealth and station by concurrence of accidents.*" [54] Yet as appealing as such a pat explanation seems, there are certain difficulties inherent in the unqualified use of such biographical data. For one thing, the over-all judicial reputations of the other four justices of humble origin—Henry Baldwin, Samuel F. Miller, Sherman Minton, and Earl Warren can hardly be accounted for by this explanation. Furthermore, a variety of other explanations involving such things as political associations, educational conditioning, or ideological commitments to nationalism or states' rights might appear just as plausible as the emphasis upon family background.

It would be a serious mistake, however, to conclude that the background factors have had no influence upon judicial behavior whatsoever. The social attitudes of families in the gentry class or professionalized upper-middle class, and particularly the traditions of the families with judicial associations, may be accounted subtle factors influencing the tone and temper of judicial decision making. While such influence cannot ordinarily be traced in cause-and-effect formulas in specific decisions, it frequently emerges in the careers of individual justices as setting implicit limits on the scope of theoretical decision-making possibilities. Justice Frankfurter once wrote that "by the very nature of the functions of the Supreme Court, each member of it is subject only to his own sense of trusteeship of what are perhaps the most revered traditions in our national system." [55] If it is in this sense that the Supreme Court is the keeper of the American conscience, it is essentially the conscience of the American upper-middle class sharpened by the imperative of individual social responsibility and political activism, and conditioned by the conservative impact of legal training and professional legal attitudes and associations.

References

1. The material in this chapter is drawn largely from an earlier article and is reproduced with the permission of the Wayne State University Press. See John R. Schmidhauser, "The Justices of the Supreme Court—A Collective Portrait," *Midwest Journal of Political Science*, III (1959), 1–57. The article contains extensive charts detailing the social and economic variations in judicial selection and an appendix which incorporates the sources for data on each member of the Supreme Court.

2. This covers the period 1789 through 1959. The total includes John Rutledge, who actually served, under a recess appointment, as Chief Justice, but failed to secure Senate confirmation. Individuals who were promoted from Associate to Chief Justice (White and Stone) or who received two separate appointments (Hughes) have been counted once. Individuals who were appointed but declined to serve have not been included.

3. C. Wright Mills, *The Power Elite* (New York: Oxford University Press, 1956), pp. 231–241.

4. See, for example, Arthur Schlesinger, *Political and Social History of the United States* (New York: The Macmillan Company, 1925), or Schlesinger and Dixon R. Fox (eds.), *A History of American Life* (12 vols.; New York: The Macmillan Company, 1943).

5. For discussion of the utility of these factors as determinants of social status, see the seminal work of Joseph Schneider, "Fame and Social Origin," *Social Forces*, XIV (1936), 354–361; also, Liston Pope, "Religion and the Class Structure," *Annals of the American Academy of Political and Social Science*, CCLVI (1948), 84–91; and Donald R. Matthews, *The Social Background of Political Decision-Makers* (Garden City, N.Y.: Doubleday & Company, Inc., 1954), pp. 23–29.

6. Matthews, *op. cit.*, p. 23.

7. Richard Hofstadter, *The American Political Tradition* (New York: Alfred A. Knopf, Inc., 1951), pp. 48–51.

8. Lewis Namier, *The Structure of Politics at the Accession of George III* (London: Macmillan and Company, Ltd., 1957), pp. 2–4.

9. For two fine analyses of such factors in British politics, see two articles by W. L. Guttsman, "The Changing Social Structure of the British

Political Elite, 1886–1935," *British Journal of Sociology,* II (1951), 122–134, and "Aristocracy and the Middle Class in the British Political Elite, 1886–1916," *British Journal of Sociology,* V (1954), 12–32.

10. This distinction has been dealt with in excellent fashion in Andrew Hacker's "Liberal Democracy and Social Control," *American Political Science Review,* LI (1957), 1010–1021.

11. William Cushing, Alfred Moore, Morrison R. Waite, Lucius Q. C. Lamar, Rufus W. Peckham, Edward D. White, William R. Day, Mahlon Pitney, William H. Taft, John H. Clarke, Benjamin N. Cardozo, and Potter Stewart.

12. John Jay, Samuel Nelson, David Davis, Joseph Bradley, Lucius Q. C. Lamar, and Tom C. Clark.

13. John Marshall, Brockholst Livingston, Thomas Todd, Smith Thompson, Philip P. Barbour, John A. Campbell, John Marshall Harlan (of Kentucky), David Brewer, Melville W. Fuller, Horace Gray, George Shiras, Oliver W. Holmes, William F. Moody, Joseph R. Lamar, and John Marshall Harlan (of New York).

14. Pitirim Sorokin, *Social Mobility* (New York: Harper & Brothers, 1927), p. 450.

15. Murray G. Lawson, "The Foreign-born in Congress, 1789–1949; A Statistical Summary," *American Political Science Review,* LI (1957), 1183.

16. In determining the ethnic origins of Supreme Court justices, only the predominant ethnic strain has been indicated. As might be expected in a "melting pot" society, many of the justices are of mixed ethnic strains. Individual names in themselves are not very satisfactory clues for the determination of ethnic origin. For example, Justice William Johnson of South Carolina proved to be a descendant of Dutch ancestors named Jansen.

17. See Daniel S. McHargue's detailed examination of the factors influencing the appointment of Supreme Court justices, "Appointments to the Supreme Court, 1789–1932" (Unpublished Doctoral dissertation, University of California, 1949), pp. 1–499.

18. "Report of the Committee on Linguistic and National Stocks in the Population in 1790," *Annual Report of the American Historical Society,* I (1931), 124; the most reliable data for comparison are the series of Census Bureau studies of nationality backgrounds which were begun in 1910; see, for example, "Country of Origin," *Sixteenth Census of U.S., 1940: Population* (Washington: Bureau of the Census, U.S. Department of Commerce, 1941), p. 9.

19. Hacker, *loc. cit.,* pp. 1010–1021.

20. See H. Richard Niebuhr's challenging work, *The Social Sources of Denominationalism* (New York: Holt, Rinehart and Winston, Inc., 1929).

21. See, especially, John Higham, *Strangers in the Land: Patterns of American Nativism, 1860–1929* (New Brunswick, N.J.: Rutgers University Press, 1955).

22. McHargue, *op. cit.*, pp. 443–450.

23. *Ibid.*, p. 149.

24. Quoted in *ibid.*, p. 428.

25. *Ibid.*, p. 489–499.

26. As reported in the *New York Times,* July 29, 1949, p. 1.

27. Robert K. Carr, *The Supreme Court and Judicial Review* (New York: Holt, Rinehart and Winston, Inc., 1942), p. 249.

28. Unsigned review of Alexis de Tocqueville, *Democracy in America,* in *United States Magazine and Democratic Review,* II (1838), 341–349.

29. See, for example, the perceptive treatments by Felix Frankfurter, "The Zeitgeist and the Judiciary," in Archibald MacLeish and E. F. Prichard, Jr. (eds.), *Law and Politics: Occasional Papers of Felix Frankfurter* (New York: Harcourt, Brace & Company, 1939), pp. 3–9; Benjamin R. Twiss, *Lawyers and the Constitution* (Princeton, N.J.: Princeton University Press, 1942); and C. Wright Mills, *White Collar* (New York: Oxford University Press, 1956), pp. 121–129, in the Galaxy edition.

30. McHargue, *op. cit.*, pp. 1–499.

31. Charles Warren, *The Supreme Court in United States History,* I (Boston: Little, Brown & Company, 1922), 404, note 1.

32. In his assessment of the Senate's role in the selection of Supreme Court justices, Professor Harris contended that "the increasing role of the Supreme Court in passing upon social and economic measures has led to greater attention to the philosophy, record, and attitudes of nominees on such issues, and far less concern than formerly to their party regularity." See Joseph P. Harris, *The Advice and Consent of the Senate* (Berkeley: University of California Press, 1953), p. 303. However, the Supreme Court has always passed upon constitutional questions having profound social and economic implications. Selection of Supreme Court members on the basis of ideology has been a relatively constant factor, whereas party regularity has been less significant as party affiliation and ideological commitment have tended to become unrelated.

33. James Laughlin, "Biographical Sketch of Justice Catron," *Tennessee Historical Magazine,* IV (1918), 77.

34. Francis P. Weisenburger, *The Life of John McLean* (Columbus: Ohio University Press, 1937), pp. 66–68; Carl Brent Swisher, *Roger B. Taney* (New York: The Macmillan Company, 1935), pp. 132–133.

35. Quoted in Carr, *op. cit.*, p. 238.

36. *Ibid.*, p. 239.

37. Quoted in McHargue, *op. cit.*, p. 356; italics mine.

38. McHargue, *op. cit.*, pp. 529–532.

39. By the following year electoral fortunes gave the Jacksonians control of the Senate, and another nomination of Taney, this time for the Chief Justiceship, was approved.

40. Warren, *op. cit.*, II, 259.

41. In selecting the major political occupations of the justices, the

political position which was, according to the biographical data, most clearly related to the individual's selection to the Supreme Court was chosen. Thus Justice Catron served for ten years as a Tennessee judge, but the fact that he was, for many years, one of Andrew Jackson's political managers in Tennessee was undoubtedly of greater influence in his elevation to the nation's highest court. Similarly, Justice David Davis served as an Illinois state judge for fourteen years, but his appointment to the Supreme Court was probably more attributable to his successful management of Lincoln's political campaigns at certain stages in the latter's career.

42. For a rather vague discussion of the criteria for judicial selection adopted by President Eisenhower, see William P. Rogers, "Judicial Appointments in the Eisenhower Administration," *41 Journal of the American Judicature Society* (August, 1957), 39–40.

43. Cong. Rec., 84th Cong., 2nd Sess., April 30, 1956, p. 6521.

44. 1789–1828: William Cushing, Thomas Todd, and Robert Trimble (3); 1829–1861: Robert Grier, Samuel Nelson, John Catron (3); 1861–1888: Horace Gray, Samuel Blatchford, David Davis, Stephen Fields, Ward Hunt, William Strong, William Woods (7); 1889–1919: Howell Jackson, David Brewer, Henry Brown, Rufus Peckham, Mahlon Pitney, Oliver W. Holmes, William R. Day, Horace Lurton (8); 1920–1932: Edward Sanford, Benjamin N. Cardozo (2); 1933–1959: William Brennan (1); total 24.

45. Felix Frankfurter, "The Supreme Court in the Mirror of the Justices," *105 University of Pennsylvania Law Review* (1956–1957), 791–793.

46. *Ibid.,* p. 785.

47. *Ibid.,* p. 787.

48. See, especially, Evan A. Evans, "Political Influences in the Selection of Federal Judges," *1948 Wisconsin Law Review,* pp. 330–337.

49. For an example of the influence of railroad magnates and corporation executives, see John P. Frank, "The Appointment of Supreme Court Justices: Prestige, Principles and Politics," *1941 Wisconsin Law Review,* pp. 179–180.

50. Frankfurter, "The Supreme Court in the Mirror of the Justices," p. 784.

51. See, for example, Richard Hofstadter, *The Age of Reform* (New York: Alfred A. Knopf, Inc., 1955), pp. 215–216.

52. For several examples of the intervention of corporation officials in the appointing process, see John P. Frank's analysis (presented in three installments), *loc. cit.,* pp. 172, 343, 461.

53. The over-all judicial reputations of individual justices are admittedly imprecise but, pending a more intensive study, may be utilized to demonstrate the nature of the problem.

54. Laughlin, *op. cit.,* p. 77; italics mine.

55. Felix Frankfurter, "The Administrative Side of Chief Justice Hughes," *63 Harvard Law Review* (1949–1950), 4.

———— II

The External Forces Operating

upon the Supreme Court

_____ *4*

Lawyers, Judges, and
Their Professional Associations

IT HAS LONG been recognized that lawyers, in presenting arguments before the Supreme Court of the United States, may influence in an important manner the development of American constitutional law.[1] Further, the judicial reasoning of respected federal and state judges may achieve a high receptivity among the Supreme Court justices.[2] Little attention has been paid, however, to the subtle external influences which may be brought to bear upon the federal justices in their frequent contacts with lawyers and federal and state judges in the professional associations in which they commonly participate. Some of these associations are of a formal, public nature, involving such official obligations as presiding over the federal judicial conferences.[3] Others are informal, such as the customary attendance and participation in the annual meetings of the American Bar Association.

Since the founding of the American Bar Association in the nineteenth century, a great many of the members of the Supreme Court have devoted time and energy to it. For some, such as George Sutherland and William Howard Taft, this activity represented merely a continuation of the kind of participation they had engaged in before their appointments to the Supreme Court. As former leaders of the ABA, they partook, not as critics, but as initiates. Others, like Louis Brandeis and Harlan Fiske Stone, undertook roles designed to evoke in members of the legal profession a greater sense of social responsibility. And one cannot relegate efforts of the latter sort to the past. Recently, Justice Felix Frankfurter, in his dissenting opinion in *Ferguson* v. *Moore–McCormack Lines, Inc.*, made the following comment:

> It deserves to be recorded that Professor John Chipman Gray, a legal scholar with social insight, taught his students fifty years ago, before the first workmen's compensation law had been enacted, that it is anachronistic to apply the common-law doctrine of negligence to injuries suffered by railroad employees rather than have society recognize such injuries as inevitable incidents of railroading and provide compensation on that basis. The persistence of this archaic and cruel system is attributable to many factors. Inertia of course. But also it is merely one illustration of the lag of reform because of the opposition of lawyers who resist change of the familiar, particularly when they have thriven under some outworn doctrine of law.[4]

Chief Justice Earl Warren's termination of membership in the American Bar Association thus represents a dramatic exception to a normally close relationship.[5] Most of the biographical treatments of this relationship emphasize the efforts of individual members of the Supreme Court with respect to the organized bar. It is the primary purpose of this chapter to reverse the coin, to examine the efforts of the American Bar Association and related professional organizations to influence, with respect to decision making, the justices of the Supreme Court of the United States. Particular attention will be paid to the professional criticism of the Warren Court's decision making in federal-state relations.

The Warren Court and Its "Literate" Critics

Perhaps the single most dramatic act relating to the contemporary prestige and influence of the Warren Court in federal-state relations occurred in August, 1958. It was then that the Conference of State Chief Justices adopted a resolution urging the federal Supreme Court to exercise judicial self-restraint in dealing with the problems of federalism. The resolution stated that the "system of federalism . . . is sound and should be more diligently preserved." [6] The chief justices of the state supreme courts may properly be counted among the "literate" [7] critics of the federal Supreme Court. Furthermore, the split between those who supported and those who opposed this resolution was not along regional geographic lines. Significant numbers of northern and western chief justices supported the critical resolution.[8]

What factors contributed to this state of affairs? Has the Warren Court's conception of its role in American federalism been strikingly different from earlier conceptions? Have the justices of the Warren Court departed so radically from the traditional behavior patterns of American judges that they have been deservedly stripped of the deference which has customarily been accorded to members of the Supreme Court? Have the state supreme courts been staffed with justices who, in the contemporary scene, are qualitatively superior to the federal justices?

The highest state appellate courts, particularly those whose traditions antedate the Supreme Court of the United States, have produced eminent jurists such as Kent, Parsons, Shaw, Ruffin, Cooley, Holmes, and Cardozo. On occasion, such state judges have asserted the kind of self-assurance which Holmes exemplified in one of his early letters to Sir Frederick Pollack. In 1891, while an Associate Justice of the Supreme Judicial Court of Massachusetts, he wrote,

I . . . send you by mail, an opinion of mine reported in 146 Mass. 545, which has lately been reversed by the Supreme Court of the U.S., together with [Lucius] Lamar's opinion. It is the only case written by me and almost the only one I've sat in for these 9 years that has gone to the Supreme Court . . . I think it is an interesting case and one which I could have written the other way, but I confess I think the ground adopted by the U.S. Court one which is quite irreconcilable with primary juridical notions. My view (you will see there was a dissent) carried the Supreme Court of Maine which has been tending the other way and the Court of Errors and Appeals in New York. So that in everything but technical authority the weight is on my side.[9]

The circumstances which led to the critical resolution of August, 1958, did not arise from the sort of situation which evoked Holmes' private comment. The state supreme courts have not suddenly developed a whole generation of Holmes and Cardozos. Similarly, the caliber of the justices of the national Supreme Court has not changed radically since the appointees of Roosevelt, Truman, and Eisenhower have controlled this tribunal.[10] Despite some contemporary concern over the propensity of the modern justices explicitly to express doubts in concurring and dissenting opinions which traditionally were often submerged in outwardly unified majority opinions,[11] the manner in which the justices of the Supreme Court perform their duties does not differ significantly from the behavior patterns of other American judges, past or present.

It is quite clear, however, that the action taken by the Conference of State Chief Justices is at variance with the frequently stated notion that the national courts, and particularly the Supreme Court of the United States, have had greater prestige than the courts of the states. An early and very influential statement of this notion by Chancellor James Kent emphasized differences in the quality of judges which were purportedly produced by differences in the mode of selection and stability of tenure:

> The judiciary of the United States has an advantage over many of the State Courts, in the tenure of office of the Judges, and the liberal and stable provision for their support. The United States are, by these means, fairly entitled to command better talents, and to look for more firmness of purpose, greater independence of action, and brighter displays of learning. The federal administration of justice has a manifest superiority over that of the individual states, in consequence of the uniformity of its decisions, and the universality of its application. Every state court will naturally be disposed to borrow light and aid from the national courts, rather than from the courts of other individual states, which will probably never be so generally respected and understood.[12]

One suspects that in the context of the early nineteenth century there was a stronger element of wishful thinking in Chancellor Kent's concluding sentence than the positive mode would indicate. Clearly, Kent eschewed comment upon the contemporary public policy considerations which may have "disposed" a state court "to borrow light and aid" from either the courts of another state or those of the nation.

Judgments concerning the quality of decision making are often inexorably bound up with subjective approval or disapproval of the ideological values and public policy positions of particular judges. For example, Holmes felt that Chief Justice Shaw was a great judge because he had an "appreciation of the requirements of the community. . . . few have lived who were his equals in their understanding of the grounds of public policy to which all laws must be ultimately referred." [13] Similarly, the relative prestige and influence of the state and national courts undoubtedly were in Kent's era and are today determined as much by public policy considerations as by estimates about the quality of judicial personnel. With respect to the barrage of contemporary criticism of the Supreme Court of the United States, it seems clear that public policy considerations have been a primary ingredient. This in itself is not unusual. What is striking, however, is the unique combination of circumstances that has contributed to this crisis. Not only has the Supreme Court of the United States fulfilled a new social role, but the other major political institutions of federalism have also shifted from historic patterns of public policy making to fundamentally different social roles.

In perspective, the basic changes in the social roles of the state legislatures, the state courts, and the Supreme Court of the United States are illustrative of the operation of several factors in American federalism that have been determinative since 1789. Although much emphasis has been placed upon the seemingly endless conflicts between localism and centralism, it is noteworthy that powerful social forces—whether embodied in the ascendant nationalism of the gentry class prior to 1800 or in the impatient drive of the new commercial and industrial power in the 1830's and thereafter—have operated upon the nation and upon the individual states simultaneously. The nineteenth-century shaping of public policy concerning the organization and purpose of the corporation by the state legislatures, and the establishment by the federal courts of doctrines designed to protect the interstate expansion of corporate trade and finance capital were, in a sense, reverse sides of the same coin. Willard Hurst perceptively captured the unifying elements present in state legislative and federal judicial policy in his characterization of both of these tendencies as designed to release private energy in order to utilize and exploit a rich material environment.[14]

It would be a mistake, however, to assume that the political institutions of American federalism have been affected by such broad social tendencies in the same way. To the extent that particular institutions were responsive to the demands of the emerging commercial and industrial forces, these institutions acquired greater prestige and influence. Conversely, institutions which attempted to thwart such demands were destined to decline in public esteem and importance. The relation between the thrust and drive of particular social, economic, and political forces and the tendency for the political institutions of American federalism to flourish or atrophy is especially important in the institutional evolution of the national judicial system, the state judicial systems, and the state legislatures.

The basic area of disagreement which was frequently at the heart of the dramatic nineteenth-century constitutional conflicts between the nation and the states concerned the fundamental question of the extent to which public authority may restrain private economic activity in order to protect the public interest. For much of its institutional history until 1937, the Supreme Court of the United States fulfilled a social role which attracted the support of interests and groups which tended to emphasize private economic freedom against public control or regulation. The Supreme Court's abandonment of this role after 1937 has lost to it much of the influential support of such interests, a transition which serves in large part to explain the characteristics of the contemporary "crisis." An historical examination of the social roles of the federal courts, the state legislatures, and the state courts may serve to illustrate this loss of interest-group support clearly.

The Historic Setting of the Problem

The courts of the nation, from the very beginning of the federal system in 1789, became identified as institutions which were more reliable as defenders of private property than were most of the courts of the states. In part this identification resulted from the fact that the federal courts were the constitutionally ordained appliers of the limitation upon state actions which impaired the obligation of a contract. It is equally true, however, that the justices, particularly during the Marshall era, exhibited unseemly enthusiasm for this task. The framers of the Constitution had, after all, conceived the contract clause as a protection of the sanctity of private contracts. But the judicial protagonists of the doctrine of vested property rights, under the intellectual leadership of Chief Justice John Marshall and Justice Joseph Story, broadened the constitutional definition of the word "contract" to include public grants, corporate charters, and state legislative enactments which exempted particular tracts of land from state taxation.[15]

In the period of American history before the Civil War, and, in fact, for some time thereafter, the chief responsibility for the social regulation of property rights, corporate or otherwise, was exercised by the state governments. The state governments vigorously promoted economic development through public works such as canals, the granting of tax exemptions to new industries, and the granting of subsidies.[16] That adequate regulation in the public interest should accompany economic promotion by the state governments was keenly recognized by many state political leaders. Ironically, many of the battles for adequate state regulation and taxation of economic enterprise in the Jacksonian era were won in the state legislatures and the state courts but were ultimately lost before the Supreme Court of the United States.[17] The chief avenues of escape from state regulation lay in the invocation of the contract clause of the national Constitution or in the establishment of national court jurisdiction as an alternative to the occasionally hostile state court systems. It is important to note that the death of Chief Justice Marshall brought no fundamental change in this relation.

To some extent the Taney Court contract-clause decisions broadened the scope of state economic autonomy, but the effect of such decision making was at best ambiguous. With respect to the expansion of the jurisdiction of the national courts, the Taney Court laid the groundwork for the rather complete erosion of state regulatory authority which took place after the Civil War. In 1844 the Taney Court ruled that corporations could be included within the meaning of the word "citizen" in diversity-of-state citizenship cases arising under Article III of the Constitution.[18] This and similar rulings opened the floodgates for corporate litigation before the national courts. In 1840 only 92 cases were pending before the Supreme Court; by 1850 the number rose to 253 cases; by 1860 to 310 cases. After the Civil War, the general corporate desire to avoid the state judicial systems was given impetus by congressional approval of legislation broadening the scope of national judicial authority to encompass virtually every claimed federal right. The total number of cases pending before the Supreme Court catapulted from 310 in 1860 to 636 cases in 1870, 1,212 cases in 1880, and 1,816 cases in 1890.[19]

Justice John Archibald Campbell, in a number of dissenting opinions in the 1850's, presented a classic appraisal of the impact of corporate power and influence upon the social and political fabric of the states. State governments were endangered by corporations whose "revenues and establishments mock at the frugal and stinted conditions of state administration; [whose] pretensions and demands are sovereign, admitting, impatiently interference by state authority." [20] Ethically, corporation directors were motivated by "a love of power, a preference for corporate interests to moral or political principles or public duties, and an antagonism to individual freedom. . . ." The doctrine of the Letson case extending the jurisdiction of national courts to make for greater access by corporations would, stated Campbell, tend to "establish on the soil of every state a caste made up of combinations of men for the most part under the most favorable conditions of society, who will habitually look beyond the institutions and authorities of state, to the central government for the strength and support necessary to maintain them in the enjoyment of their special privileges and exemptions." [21] Campbell's analysis prophetically described the era of the "Robber Barons" and the view of contemporary America etched by C. Wright Mills in *The Power Elite*.

The Post-Civil War Era

The degradation of state political institutions which took place during the post-Civil War period was only one aspect of a change taking place throughout American society. Fundamentally, the ideology of the emerging industrial and professional leadership represented a radical departure from that of the declining gentry class. The leaders of the older mercantile and agrarian gentry class had often disagreed over the question which government(s), that of the nation or those of states, should perform specific functions. But Federalists, Jeffersonian Republicans and for the most part Jacksonian Democrats viewed public service based on educational attainment and civic virtue as a primary social obligation. This tradition, which was gradually eroding during the period 1830–1860, disintegrated after the Civil War. The emerging business and professional elite was more prone to concentration upon private affairs, largely eschewing the older tradition of public service based on civic virtue. Moreover, the spirit and temper of the post-Civil War era emphasized private rather than public initiative. If the Civil War was a crisis of federalism which tested the power of the government of the nation to curtail the separatist tendencies of an entire region, the crisis in the period 1888–1936 may be viewed as one in which the power of *any* government in the United States to regulate and control the economy in the public interest was sternly tested.

The state legislatures continued, on occasion, to try to reassert in meaningful fashion their earlier role as regulators of economic and social affairs. The populist and Progressive movements sometimes achieved marked regional gains. But local pressures from strong lobbies backed by economically powerful corporations often corrupted entire legislative bodies. Furthermore, social experimentation which was considered antithetical to the ascendant corporate power was often discouraged not only by the private groups operating to control state politics but by the national courts as well. In this sense national judicial umpiring of federalism seriously weakened the capacity of the states to regulate in the midst of a period when industrialization and urbanization made such regulation imperative.[22] Social forces within the states as well as national judicial restrictions upon the states combined to erode the capacity of the states to regulate effectively in the public interest. Where in the 1830's the state legislatures reflected the vigor and self-confidence of an optimistic agrarian yeomanry buttressed by the artisans in the small cities, the 1930's generally found the state legislatures dominated by grossly overrepresented farmers and small-town dwellers whose retention of political power was not matched by economic independence or buoyant confidence in the future.[23] In the contemporary setting, state social experimentation usually reflects the ascendancy of private over public government. The prototype of the acceptable social experiment is Delaware's approach to the chartering and regulation of corporations rather than Wisconsin's workmen's compensation and unemployment relief legislation. Whereas in the Age of Jackson the state legislatures addressed themselves to the promotion of economic development and the serious appraisal of the social as well as economic implications of the new commercial and industrial corporations, today in contemporary America it is the corporations which address themselves to the problems of state and local governmental reform. Governmental reform is frequently considered a secondary, albeit necessary, adjunct of private regional economic development.[24] In short, the political institutions of the states were, by the 1930's and thereafter, fulfilling public policy roles quite different from those of earlier historic periods.

The declining regulatory vigor of the states in the first three decades of the twentieth century was counterbalanced to some extent by a greater assumption of regulatory responsibility by the national government. During the Presidency of Theodore

Roosevelt, two major approaches to the development of national regulatory authority were seriously considered. These efforts at national regulation were largely stimulated by the fact that decisions in behalf of laissez faire by the Supreme Court created a "twilight zone" in American federalism in which corporations were frequently able to operate free from either state or national supervision. Theodore Roosevelt reasserted the doctrine of one of the founding fathers, James Wilson, that the national government could exercise power necessary to cope with any problem which the states were incapable of handling. Even when direct constitutional authority was lacking, the power to act in such situations was one inherent in national sovereignty. When Roosevelt's Attorney General, Charles Bonaparte, proposed this doctrine in the case of *Kansas* v. *Colorado*,[25] the Supreme Court rejected it decisively. Congress, during the same period did, however, achieve partial success in developing the concept of a "federal police power." The national Congress invoked its constitutionally enumerated powers, particularly over interstate and foreign commerce, taxation, and postal services, in order to prohibit crime and immorality and to provide some legislation dealing with the health and welfare of underprivileged groups in society. However, until the late 1930's, political circumstances and federal judicial conservatism effectively barred widespread national activity of this sort.

The Contemporary Setting of the Problem

It has often been argued that the future of the political institutions of American federalism is inexorably bound up with the successes and failures of the powerful interest groups which compete for economic advantage and political power. It is quite clear that few contemporary groups are inclined to identify themselves permanently with a particular set of political institutions, as was rather evident in the Calhounian association of property rights in slavery and the doctrines of state nullification and secession. In general, each group seeks fulfillment of its objectives through whatever institution may seem best suited for the task. However, in the contemporary setting, it is equally clear that there are a number of private centers of economic power for whom the invocation of states' rights serves as a lever for the avoidance of effective public regulation and social responsibility. Conversely, there are other interest groups which look primarily to the national government to fulfill needs which have long been neglected by the political institutions of the states.

One may identify the direction taken by these competing forces by contrasting the views presented by the NAM and the CIO. In 1952, the National Association of Manufacturers argued from a modern states' rights position which has been represented in Congress by a highly effective conservative southern Democratic and northern Republican coalition. "Unless the trend toward even bigger government is halted, and until it is reversed, the states and private business alike face the prospect of ultimate, complete domination by the federal government." [26] In the same year a spokesman for the CIO, Frank Fernbach, articulated the urban-labor position in these terms:

> Democracy is being stultified in the 48 states by an inequitable system of representation which, in varying degrees, disenfranchises the urban-labor voter. Under the imperfect structures of both our federal and state governments, labor can at least hope for a more equitable representation in Washington than in most of the rural-county dominated capitals of the states. As a consequence, even issues which should be susceptible to intelligent and vigorous action in the states—mine safety and inspection, for example, must be brought by labor to the federal government for action.[27]

He might well have added that of the two chambers of Congress, the House of Representatives has, in modern times, become more susceptible than the Senate to the forces which dominate the state legislatures. Because congressional districts are created by the state legislatures, the national congressmen have been more conspicuous advocates of anti-regulatory states' rights than the senators have. The latter, being elected at large in each state, more frequently represent the pro-positive government electorate of the large metropolitan centers.

A revealing demonstration of the effectiveness with which nationally organized interest groups attempt to utilize the political institutions of American federalism for their special purposes is provided by the contemporary efforts of the leaders of the American Bar Association with respect to the relative influence and prestige of the federal Supreme Court and the supreme courts of the states. The public policy positions of the leaders of the American Bar Association are of significance in three important respects. First, the leadership of the Association has often provided the most articulate statements of the modern states' rights position. Secondly, the American Bar Association has been especially influential in molding public attitudes toward national and state judicial institutions because the recommendations of the ABA's leaders are often treated by the mass media as the dispassionate judgments of personally disinterested experts. Thirdly, the viewpoints and tactics of the leaders of the American Bar Association have especial relevance for the contemporary "crisis" of the Supreme Court of the United States.

In contemporary America, the size and complexity of the bar defy simple categorization, but the American Bar Association is comprised of a group whose programs and ideological predilections are a matter of public record. The main thrust of the public policy stands of the American Bar Association has been exemplified in its opposition to the Child Labor Amendment, to the Roosevelt Court Reform Bill, to the Wagner-Murray-Dingell (National Health Insurance) Bill, to the Genocide Convention and the Covenant on Human Rights, to the Ewing Health Bill, the Gore-Holifield Bill (providing for public development of atomic energy for peacetime purposes), and to having an ABA observer with the United States delegation to the United Nations. The programs it supported are equally indicative. Since 1937, the American Bar Association was for the Walter-Logan Bill, the Tidelands Oil Bill, the Mundt-Nixon (Internal Security) Bill, the Reed-Dirksen Amendment (placing a 25 per cent limit on income tax except under certain conditions), the Bricker Amendment, the Jenkins-Keogh (lawyers' tax benefits) Bill, the Wham resolutions (in effect urging [a] Congress to guard against leaving interpretation involving states' rights to the Supreme Court and [b] urging transferal of many functions such as urban renewal to the states), and Congressional legislation designed to override recent Supreme Court decisions involving basic procedural rights.[28] The latest stand of the ABA House of Delegates on internal security is not the first of its kind. In 1952, the House of Delegates approved a resolution commending the House Un-American Activities Committee and the Senate Internal Security Sub-Committee on the manner in which they conducted their hearings and investigations. The House also approved an amendment to this resolution submitted by Charles Rhyne to extend this commendation to the McCarthy Subcommittee for "conducting its inquiry in the exposition [sic] of Communist activities in a dignified lawyerlike way, with full recognition of all the constitutional rights of those they call before them." [29]

Recently Frederick Bernays Wiener deplored the fact that bestowal of the American Bar Association Gold Medal for Conspicuous Service had become a prize for past presidents, whereas in earlier days it was reserved for men of the stature of Holmes, Hughes, or Williston.[30] The bestowal of the Medal upon Frank E. Holman in 1953 "for his work in rousing the country to the dangers of international treaties which may infringe upon freedoms guaranteed by the Bill of Rights" [31] would abundantly bear out Wiener's charge.

In the light of its public policy positions since 1937, what has been the role of the American Bar Association with respect to the federal Supreme Court and the highest appellate courts of the states?

The ABA, the Federal Supreme Court, and States' Rights

Prior to 1939, the American Bar Association was perhaps the most consistent and dedicated supporter of the federal judiciary and especially the Supreme Court of the United States. In the battle over Franklin Roosevelt's Court Reform Bill in 1937, the Association not only marshaled the support of most lawyers against the bill but played an effective role in influencing congressional and public opinion against it as well. Traditionally, although it cultivated good relations with the state judiciaries, the leadership of the American Bar Association clearly felt that the important economic interests and ideological values were more reliably safeguarded by the federal courts. One facet of the traditional ABA viewpoint was enunciated by William Howard Taft very explicitly in 1922. Addressing the American Bar Association, Taft pointed out:

> Litigants from the eastern part of the country who are expected to invest their capital in the West or South will hardly concede the proposition that their interests as creditors will be as sure of impartial consideration in a Western or a Southern state court as in a federal court . . . . No single element in our governmental system has done so much to secure capital for the legitimate development of enterprise throughout the West and South as the existence of federal courts there, with a jurisdiction to hear diverse citizenship cases.[32]

The identification of the national courts as more reliable bulwarks of anti-regulatory ideas or as more stable defenders of creditor's interests than the highest state appellate courts persisted long after this distinction lost much of its foundation in fact. But, as Taft's speech indicated, the image of the state courts as institutions prone to instability or radical doctrine died hard. In fact, Taft's sentiments were quoted approvingly and elaborated upon in 1938 by Judge John J. Parker.[33]

Of course, it had been historically true that, on occasion, some state courts fulfilled social roles similar to that of the national courts from the very outset of American federalism. Further, the researches of Edward Corwin, Wallace Mendelson, Leonard Levy, and Monrad Paulsen indicate that some of the state courts pioneered in the development of judicial doctrines which seriously curtailed the ability of the legislatures to control economic license or upheld violations of noneconomic freedom and racial equality.[34] But, of far greater importance, the social role of the state courts had, by the 1930's, changed appreciably in the century since the ascendancy of Jacksonian Democracy.

The practice of popular election of judges, which had been adopted in many states before the Civil War, became by custom a popular ratification of the nominees of conservatively oriented state or local bar associations. Social trends within even the more recently settled trans-Mississippi Western states suggest that by the mid-twentieth century, the judges of the highest state appellate courts are apt to be elderly lawyers whose professional training was more systematic than that of the judges of earlier generations. These modern state judges appear to be slightly less politically oriented than their predecessors. But this statement is true only in the sense that a few more state judges have eschewed public political activity than in earlier times. Most, however, have been heavily involved in the kind of private organizational and ideological politics which has been a characteristic function of the national, state, and local bar associations.[35] No longer are the state appellate courts apt to be hostile to the interests of corporations and property. Politically, the state supreme courts are often susceptible to the same social forces which have transformed the state legislatures from bulwarks of a self-confident agrarian yeomanry in the 1830's to bulwarks of anti-regulatory reaction in modern times.

The gradual change in the social role of the state supreme courts did not shake the primary reliance by the leaders of the American Bar Association upon the federal Supreme Court until the great changes in constitutional interpretation made in the late 1930's. After 1937, the Supreme Court's traditional role as protector of economic freedom against encroachment by either the nation or the states was virtually abandoned. Conversely, certain basic noneconomic freedoms involving speech, press, religion, and assembly have been protected against state action through doctrinal broadening of the scope of the due process clause of the Fourteenth Amendment as well as through meaningful application of the equal protection clause to the realities of racial discrimination in education and transportation. A typical statement indicating the extent of the withdrawal of the national Supreme Court from the economic affairs of the states is found in *Lee Optical Company* v. *Williamson*.

The day is gone when this Court uses the Due Process Clause of the Fourteenth Amendment to strike down state laws regulatory of business and industrial conditions because they may be unwise, improvident, or out of harmony with a particular school of thought . . . "for protection against abuses by legislatures, the people must resort to the polls, not the courts." [36]

The reaction of the leaders of the American Bar Association to the doctrinal developments immediately after 1937 was strong. ABA President Frank Hogan, in a major address before the ABA Assembly in 1939, deplored these decision-making tendencies as an abandonment of economic freedoms and states' rights to the national legislative will.[37] An *American Bar Association Journal* editorial stated, in the same year, that,

in the face of trends which leave the Tenth Amendment rarely mentioned in constitutional interpretation, the ABA will abundantly justify its existence and will deserve the support of all lawyers and citizens, if through it the organized Bar can make some substantial contribution to the defense and maintenance of the Bill of Rights intact.[38]

The ABA's Committee on Judicial Salaries, which heretofore had favored an increase, coldly suggested that salary increases for federal judges be deferred until the federal budget is balanced. The Committee's resolution was approved by the House of Delegates.[39]

The tone and temper of ABA feelings about the New Deal judges and justices were probably accurately reflected in the tart remarks made before the Committee on Judicial Salaries by delegates A. G. C. Bierer and [Idaho judge] James F. Ailshie. Bierer stated that "it should be more the concern of this Association to worry less about getting adequate compensation for the judges and more about getting adequate judges for the compensation." Judge Ailshie argued that "more than half of the federal judges who have been appointed within the last quarter of a century are getting a better salary today than they ever earned in the practice of the law." [40] In contrast to the increasing disenchantment with the federal judiciary was the *American Bar*

Association Journal editorial on the Tompkins decision: "If the genesis of the doctrine [of *Swift* v. *Tyson*] was a lack of confidence in the scholarship and ability of the state judges in our pioneer days, the abandonment of the doctrine may well be considered proof of confidence restored." [41]

The continuing prospect of federal Supreme Court doctrinal changes soon brought a fundamental shift in attitude in the American Bar Association. In an address to the Illinois State Bar Association on November 28, 1941, ABA President Walter P. Armstrong virtually spelled out a new litigatory and doctrinal strategy for lawyers and state judges seeking to neutralize or defeat the doctrinal tendencies of the New Deal Court. Couching his suggestions in the form of predictions, Armstrong stated that

> . . . a great state supreme court, construing the Federal Constitution, in a case where there is no binding precedent, will not merely engage in a guessing contest as to the view that the Supreme Court of the United States will take, but will arrive at its independent conclusion and assert its own views. If this feeling of independence comes to pervade the state courts to as full an extent as I believe it will, we have a right to expect from them great opinions expounding the Federal Constitution—opinions that will challenge the attention of the nation and materially influence the development of constitutional law.
>
> The effect will by no means stop there. The construction of its own constitution by a state supreme court is, of course, conclusive in the Supreme Court of the United States. None the less, even here, the Supreme Court of the United States has wielded great influence. Many provisions of state constitutions are identical with those of the Constitution of the United States. When such provisions have in the past been construed, state supreme courts have usually followed the construction placed by the Supreme Court of the United States on similar provisions of the Federal Constitution. Many have gone further and—sometimes contrary to their own inclination—adopted constructions of their own constitutions which they consider in line with the current tendency of the Supreme Court of the United States, even though that court has not passed on the question. *Here, too, in the future we may expect a greater independence on the part of the state supreme courts.*

> *Already cases are arising where rights are asserted under provisions of state constitutions similar to clauses of the Fourteenth Amendment and where counsel are careful not to make any claim under the Federal Constitution.*[42]

Why the State Supreme Courts?

From the ABA's standpoint, was the shift in emphasis from the national to the state courts justified? Two factors operated to confirm, in large part, Armstrong's hopes. First, the fundamental changes in the social and political structures of the states described above had, over a period of a century, transformed many of the state supreme courts into strongholds of legal conservatism. Secondly, and in ironic contrast to the frequent claims that the Supreme Court of the United States has steadily encroached upon the rights of the states, much of the post-1937 decision making of the highest federal tribunal has contributed to the prestige and influence of the state supreme courts by broadening their authority in a number of areas. The state courts were restored their autonomy with respect to common law matters.[43] Furthermore, the withdrawal of the national Supreme Court from its earlier role as supervisor of the economic policies of the states actually did not leave such supervision to the people at the polls, as was suggested in the Lee Optical decision. The state courts took this responsibility with alacrity.[44]

Although the highest state appellate courts have, of course, exercised their decision-making power to strike down blatant instances of legislative favoritism,[45] the ideological emphasis in many post-World War II state supreme court decisions involving economic affairs has been upon nineteenth-century liberalism. Fundamentally, the attitude of many of the state justices seems typified by the comment of Chief Justice George W. Maxey of the Supreme Court of Pennsylvania in 1944:

> Freedom of enterprise naturally results in economic inequalities but from *them* no people ever suffered anything remotely comparable to what they have suffered from *political oppression* when they permitted the government to become meddlesome enough to attempt to make all men economically equal.[46]

Despite the fact that the federal Supreme Court has eschewed the incorporation of particular economic theories as in-
terpretative dogma of the sort vigorously criticized by Justice
Holmes in the Lochner case, the practice is widespread among the
state supreme courts. For example, after the federal Supreme
Court had upheld a Nebraska statute fixing the fees charged by
private employment agencies,[47] the Nebraska Supreme Court
held the same law unconstitutional as a violation of due process
of law. Opponents of the statute had carefully based their new
challenge on the state constitution and avoided raising a federal
question. The Nebraska Court stated that the statute

> . . . has the . . . effect of substituting human judgment for the
> market place, and the judgment of individuals has never proved
> to be an adequate substitute for supply and demand. . . . The
> stifling of a legitimate occupational pursuit by price fixing has
> been condemned as unconstitutional by this court as being beyond
> the realm of a regulatory statute. . . . We find no reason for
> receding from this position.[48]

Doctrines such as liberty of contract and business affected
with a public interest which had often been invoked by the
federal Supreme Court before the 1930's have retained their
vitality in many state courts since World War II. The penchant
for the substitution of judicial for legislative wisdom concerning the broad public policy implications of state statutes is
nowhere more clearly illustrated than in two cases involving the
requirement of licensing for persons in service industries. The
Supreme Court of North Carolina, in striking down a licensing
requirement for dry cleaners, stated,

> Resort to the police power to exclude persons from an ordinary
> calling, finding justification only by the existence of a vague public
> interest, often amounting to no more than a doubtful social con-
> venience, is collectivistic in principle, destructive to the historical
> values of these guaranties, and contrary to the genius of the peo-
> ple. . . . A departure from these standards may be regarded as
> social retrogression. No good can come to society from a policy
> which tends to drive its members from the ranks of the inde-

pendently employed into the ranks of those industrially dependent, and the economic fallacy of such a policy is too obvious for comment.[49]

In holding void a state law requiring the licensing of photographers in 1946, the highest appellate court of Virginia stated,

> In this day of bureaucracies multiplied we are constrained to emphasize a firm adherence to the philosophy that that state is best governed which is least governed.[50]

It will come as a considerable surprise to those who especially enjoyed the scene in O'Connor's *Last Hurrah* in which Sheffington outwitted the unscrupulous mortician to discover that the General Court of Massachusetts cannot prohibit crematory corporations from selling memorial monuments. The Supreme Judicial Court of Massachusetts advised the legislators that a prohibition of this sort would deprive such corporations of constitutional rights. The Court added,

> [It is] fanciful rather than real [to suggest] that a bereaved family seeking a place to bury their dead might possibly be exposed to undesirable importunity in the matter of purchase of a monument or might be discriminated against for refusal to buy. . . .[51]

It is noteworthy that only rarely has a state supreme court held void a statute imposing controls upon labor unions. In virtually every instance of this kind the invalidation turned on invocation of the federal constitution under doctrines such as Thornhill.[52]

The field of public utilities rate making offers another example of the tendency of some state supreme courts to give continued vitality to doctrines which have been abandoned or considerably modified by the federal Supreme Court. In 1944, in a concurring opinion in *Federal Power Commission* v. *Natural Gas Pipeline Company,* Justice Black, supported by Justices Douglas and Murphy, stated,

> We think this an appropriate occasion to lay the ghost of *Smyth* v. *Ames* . . . which has haunted utility regulation since 1898.

It was generally felt that the Hope decision of 1944 did just that. In 1957, Justice Robert Larson of the Iowa Supreme Court applied the "fair-value" formula of *Smyth* v. *Ames,* adopting as the rate-base ratio 70 per cent for reproduction costs and 30 per cent for original costs. This ratio placed the full burden of contemporary inflation costs upon the consumer. Justice Larson stated, in answer to implied criticism of the invocation of the doctrine of 1898,

> No court should be concerned with whether it is "modern" but with whether it is right. There are such things as eternal virtues and ultimate truths, particularly in the field of constitutional law.[53]

The tendency of many of the highest appellate courts of the states to apply, in the 1940's and 1950's, laissez-faire doctrines which had been repudiated by the federal Supreme Court after 1937 was matched by a correspondingly slighter regard for the noneconomic liberties.[54] Some Southern courts have, of course, taken militantly anti-civil libertarian doctrinal positions based upon social theories such as that enunciated by the Virginia Supreme Court of Appeals in the Naim case. The Virginia court stated that

> . . . the natural law which forbids [racial] intermarriage and the social amalgamation which leads to a corruption of races is as clearly divine as that which imparted to them different natures. . . . The Fourteenth Amendment does not prohibit the state to regulate the marriage relation so that it shall not have a mongrel breed of citizens. . . . Both sacred and secular history teach that nations and races have better advanced in human progress when they cultivated their own distinctive characteristics and culture and developed their own peculiar genius.[55]

While most of the state judges outside the region would not be apt to hold social views typical of the antebellum South, they have often tended to place far less emphasis upon the noneconomic freedoms than have the justices of the Supreme Court of the United States. The old Jeffersonian conception of the states as the primary defenders of civil liberties, which was basic to the Virginia and Kentucky Resolutions of the 1790's, is clearly not applicable to the state legislatures and courts in the mid-twentieth century. Some of the most serious infringements of civil liberties in the post-World War II period were committed by state legislatures and condoned by state supreme courts in the field of subversion.[56] The administration of criminal justice by the states has often been characterized by formal and customary procedures which were violative of elementary requirements of due process. It has been generally acknowledged that truly meaningful improvements of these procedures have come primarily through intervention by the federal Supreme Court.[57] Some state justices have felt that such intervention was wholesome,[58] but in general the reaction has been critical.[59]

Perhaps the clearest illustration of the ideological penchant of some non-Southern state justices to treat problems of racial discrimination as secondary to economic interests is provided in the priority of social values indicated in *Rice* v. *Sioux City Memorial Park Cemetary*.[60] Justice Larson, for a unanimous court, attempted to distinguish the Rice case from *Shelley* v. *Kraemer*. After holding that the denial of Mrs. Rice's appeal was not state action upholding a private restrictive covenant, Justice Larson stated

> It may be desirable to hold that state action can be discerned in any case where the state has tolerated discrimination by inaction. . . . But there is a danger in attempting to remedy by such constitutional expansion. Invocation of the Constitution then might depend upon a balance of two asserted values—the privilege of the corporation and the right of the plaintiff to equality of treatment . . . it is just and proper that state authorities furnish appropriate means of extending these moral rights . . . rather than to try an extension of the coverage of the Fourteenth Amendment to fields that will abridge other individual rights and violate other constitutional guaranties.[61]

The contemporary doctrinal tendencies in many of the state supreme courts bear a striking resemblance to the decision-making tendencies of the Supreme Court of the United States before 1937. In short, ABA President Armstrong had demonstrated keen understanding of the judicial realities when he suggested greater reliance upon the state supreme courts.

The Contemporary Efforts of the ABA

In the post-World War II era, many of the leaders of the American Bar Association accepted the United Nations Organization as an international necessity but never really overcame their misgivings about most features of the New Deal or its successor, the Fair Deal. Virtually every annual presidential address and a galaxy of *American Bar Association Journal* editorials reiterated the theme that the domestic economic regulations enacted since 1933 were making the United States a regimented nation by weakening free enterprise and states' rights. Just as one may find sonorous extolling of the "eternal [economic] virtues" by some of the state supreme court justices, so can one find, with frequency, similar statements by the leaders of the American Bar Association. Thus Frank E. Holman argued that

> the laws that operate in the realm of government are as inevitable and immutable as the law of nature itself, and no nation nor its citizens can escape the operation of these laws. You cannot have a society of free men under a regimented economy. That is as certain as the law of gravitation.

In the same vein, Congressman Hatton W. Sumners, in an article entitled "The American Capacity for Self-Government Is Being Destroyed by Bureaucracy," stated,

> We cannot do to our democracy that which under the laws of cause and effect is destructive of democracy, and expect ours to survive. Governments are not accidents. They have been provided for in the great economy, and are themselves governed by natural law.[62]

When President Joseph Henderson criticized New Deal tendencies in his annual address in 1944 he added, significantly, the comment that "much of the very legislation we have criticized has already been or would very likely be upheld in the courts as constitutional." [63]

As Henderson's comment indicated, a good deal of the bitterness against the Roosevelt legislation overflowed upon the justices of the Supreme Court. Attacks questioning the ability, independence, and legal philosophy of the Supreme Court justices appeared frequently in the *ABA Journal* and were given semi-official approval by favorable editorials. A representative sample in 1944 included articles by Chief Justice George Maxey of the Pennsylvania Supreme Court, Congressman Hatton W. Sumners, Frank W. Grinnell, and George Wharton Pepper.[64] The titles ranged from Sumners' "The American Capacity for Self-Government Is Being Destroyed by Bureaucracy" to Grinnell's "The New Guesspotism."

Ben W. Palmer contributed a series of articles assessing the changes in legal philosophy and internal judicial procedures which had taken place since 1937. Not only did Palmer deplore the abandonment of natural law, *stare decisis,* and unity in decision making, but he also implied that the new judicial tendencies contributed to totalitarianism. As he put it in an article entitled "Hobbes, Holmes and Hitler,"

> If totalitarianism comes to America . . . it will come through dominance in the judiciary of men who have accepted a philosophy of law that has its roots in Hobbes and its fruition in implications from the philosophy of Holmes. . . .[65]

Editorials in the *ABA Journal* contained frontal attacks on the Supreme Court Justices. In commenting on David Lawrence's suggestion, in 1947, that a constitutional amendment be adopted abandoning life tenure for federal judges and justices, the *Journal* editorialized:

> Experience has shown, we think, that the primary cause of the conditions which Mr. Lawrence deplores (ill-considered and uncertain decisions, the remote effect of which are not yet understood) has been the appointment to the bench of men who were not properly experienced and trained for judicial work and also lack the independence, the impartiality and fidelity to the judicial function which are indispensable.[66]

Another editorial critical of the justices stated that a

> full study of the reasons why private litigants, in suits involving
> Government or among themselves, accept settlements which they
> deem unwarranted by the law and the facts, rather than risk the
> uncertainties of litigation, might show some of the conditions that
> have led to decrease in the number of cases tried.[67]

The editors of the *Journal* also reprinted approvingly Senator
Alexander Wiley's letter indicating that, as chairman of the
Senate Judiciary Committee, he would give "full weight" to the
judicial selection recommendations of "recognized and respected
legal groups" rather than to "political officials." "The present
political character of the members by the federal bench is,"
stated Wiley, "grossly lopsided on the side of Democratic
Leftists. . . ." [68] From 1947 to the present the American Bar
Association has formally sought to substitute Association approval for the traditional mode of federal judicial selection.

The efforts at "improving" the quality of federal judges and
justices were balanced by deliberate organizational efforts to
enhance the prestige of the state supreme courts. Strong *ABA
Journal* editorial support was expressed for the suggestions of
Senator Pat McCarren and Associate Justice Julian P. Alexander
of the Supreme Court of Mississippi that the time had come to
start restoring to the states the power eroded during the 1930's
and early 1940's.[69] The *American Bar Association Journal* in-
augurated a series of articles describing individual state judicial
systems and eulogizing the judicial contributions of the chief
justice of each. In commenting upon this series the editor of the
Journal wrote pointedly that "several states have a number of
judges which is comparable with the entire federal judiciary
system." [70] However, the most important step taken by the
American Bar Association was the establishment in 1949 of the
Conference of State Chief Justices. The *Journal* account of the
first meeting of this organization is very instructive:

> . . . the section on Judicial Administration of the American Bar
> Association . . . recently proposed the formation of this formal
> Conference of Chief Justices. This suggestion was promptly ap-

proved by the Association's House of Delegates at its sessions in February, 1948, which authorized the Section on Judicial Administration to undertake the organization of this conference. . . .

Bearing in mind that each of these forty-eight Chief Justices is the titular leader of the entire judicial system in his own state, each system consisting of literally hundreds of courts, the aggregate power represented by this conference can well be imagined.[71]

Since its inception in 1949, the Conference of State Chief Justices has held its annual meetings in conjunction with the annual meetings of the American Bar Association.

The over-all strategy of the American Bar Association with respect to the federal Supreme Court has had several closely related facets. On one hand, the Association has attempted to maintain its traditional reverence for the Court as an institution. In this connection the ABA House of Delegates supported the Butler Amendment in 1954 and opposed the bill introduced by Senator Jenner which would have curtailed the Supreme Court appellate jurisdiction.[72] Secondly, the Association has sometimes subjected individual Court members and, more often, particular decisions to strong criticism.[73] Thirdly, it has sought to increase its influence in the selection of federal judges and justices.[74] Fourthly, it has fostered the development of organizational centers of power which have often criticized contemporary federal judicial decision making from essentially the same ideological point of view as the Association itself.[75] Fifthly, it has administered the Annual Ross Essay Contest in a manner which has elicited winning responses which have generally been ideologically congenial to the viewpoints of the ABA's leadership. The annual topic is usually announced in the form of a pointedly leading question. The topic chosen for 1959, incidentally, was "Is There Federal Encroachment on States' Rights Which Should Be Curbed?" [76]

Conclusion

What responsibility does the Warren Court itself bear for this crisis? [77] In the foreword to the *Report of the Committee on Federal-State Relationships Affected by Judicial Decisions,* it was stated that several members of the faculty of the University of Chicago Law School contributed monographs on key aspects of the problem. Perhaps the finest testimony *in behalf* of the Warren Court may be found in these monographs.[78] One cannot escape the conclusion that if the Conference of Chief Justices had taken these studies seriously it would not have adopted the resolution criticizing the federal Supreme Court. While it is true that instances of federal judicial encroachment upon state power were documented, as they have been in virtually every historical era, the over-all impression emerging in each monograph is one which credits the federal Supreme Court with intense sensitivity to the problems of maintaining state autonomy. As was pointed out, a balanced view of the way the Court has treated such problems must include consideration not only of the cases in which the Court wrote opinions but also of the multitude of instances where the Supreme Court has refrained from rendering decisions.[79]

It is ironical, indeed, to note that the 1958 Report of the Conference of Chief Justices charged that the Supreme Court of the United States "has tended to adopt the role of policy maker without judicial restraint." Virtually every state supreme court represented in this Conference indulged in the practice of substituting its own views of the desirability of economic legislation for that of the appropriate state legislature.[80] Conversely, much of the expansion of federal authority which was deplored by the Conference resulted from federal judicial deference—judicial self-restraint—to the judgment of the national Congress.

It is quite clear that the basis for the severe contemporary criticisms of the Supreme Court of the United States has not been a dispassionate appraisal of the Court's work by allegedly personally disinterested leaders of the American Bar Association and justices of the state supreme courts. Rather, much of this contemporary criticism reflects deep-seated differences in social and political values. To date it is not certain that the present members of the federal Supreme Court have been persuaded by the criticisms of the American Bar Association and the Conference of State Chief Justices. Neither is it certain that the American Bar Association has succeeded in dominating the federal judicial selection process, despite its proud boast that President Eisenhower has submitted all judicial candidates for ABA approval "since the Dallas meeting" attended by the President in August, 1956.[81] It is clear, however, that the long-range implications of possible future successes are serious.

It has often been argued that the Supreme Court's greatest defense against external pressures lay in its own institutional procedures and traditions. These internal factors may, of course, be inadequate to the task of safeguarding the appointing process from external ideological influences whether in the form of a publicly responsible political party or a publicly irresponsible private organization. The institutional procedures and customs may, however, be of profound importance in conditioning the behavior of individuals after they have been selected as members of the Court. The succeeding two chapters are devoted to an analysis of the historical evolution of, and contemporary characteristics of, these institutional procedures and traditions.

References

1. Benjamin Twiss, *Lawyers and the Constitution* (Princeton, N.J.: Princeton University Press, 1941); Clement E. Vose, "Litigation as a Form of Pressure Group Activity," *Annals of the American Academy of Political and Social Sciences*, CCCXIX (1958); and Paul A. Freund, *On Understanding the Supreme Court* (Boston: Little, Brown & Company, 1949), especially Chapter III, entitled "Judge and Company," pp. 77 ff.

2. Professor Freund discussed this with sensitivity, *op. cit.*, pp. 78–79.

3. See, for example, the comment on "The Rule Making Function and the Judicial Conference of the United States," *44 American Bar Association Journal* (1958), 42.

4. 352 U.S. 539 (1957); for sources for other references made in this paragraph, see Joel Francis Paschal, *Mr. Justice Sutherland: A Man against the State* (Princeton, N.J.: Princeton University Press, 1951); Henry F. Pringle, *The Life and Times of William Howard Taft* (2 vols.; New York: Holt, Rinehart and Winston, Inc., 1939); Alpheus T. Mason, *Brandeis: A Free Man's Life* (New York: The Viking Press, 1946), and *Harlan Fiske Stone: Pillar of the Law* (New York: The Viking Press, 1956).

5. See the comments of ABA President Ross Malone on Warren's termination, *45 American Bar Association Journal* (1959), 109.

6. *Report of the Committee on Federal-State Relationships as Affected*

by *Judicial Decisions* (Chicago, Ill.: Conference of State Chief Justices, 1958), p. 16. Throughout this study I shall use the phrase "state supreme courts" as synonymous with the highest appellate courts of the states. It is, of course, recognized that in some states the highest appellate court is not called a supreme court.

7. Although his review was published prior to the August, 1958, Conference, Professor Philip B. Kurland probably would have included the state chief justices among the literate critics; see "The Supreme Court and Its Literate Critics," *47 Yale Review* (1958), 596–599.

8. Seven of the ten state chief justices who submitted the report were from states outside the South; in the voting on the critical resolution 36 chief justices supported it, 8 opposed it, while 2 abstained and 4 were absent, *Report, op. cit.,* pp. 15–16; opposition to the resolution came from California, Rhode Island, New Jersey, Pennsylvania, Utah, Vermont, West Virginia, and Hawaii.

9. Mark De Wolfe Howe (ed.), *The Holmes-Pollock Letters,* I (Cambridge, Mass.: Harvard University Press, 1941), 40.

10. Modern selections to the Supreme Court have reflected essentially the same factors which have been important to the selection process since 1789; John R. Schmidhauser, "The Justices of the Supreme Court: A Collective Portrait," *Midwest Journal of Political Science,* III (1959), 1–57.

11. See, for example, Karl M. ZoBell, "Division of Opinion in the Supreme Court: A History of Judicial Disintegration," *44 Cornell Law Quarterly* (1958–1959), 186–214.

12. James Kent, *1 Commentaries on American Law* (5th ed., 1844), 443–444.

13. *The Common Law* (1881), p. 106.

14. James Willard Hurst, *Law and the Conditions of Freedom in the Nineteenth Century United States* (Madison: University of Wisconsin Press, 1956), pp. 1–70.

15. In *Fletcher* v. *Peck,* 6 Cranch 48 (1810), *Dartmouth College* v. *Woodward,* 4 Wheaton 250 (1819), and *New Jersey* v. *Wilson,* 7 Cranch 103 (1812), respectively.

16. For an intensive study of the economic experiences of one state, see Louis Hartz, *Economic Policy and Democratic Thought: Pennsylvania, 1776–1860* (Cambridge, Mass.: Harvard University Press, 1948).

17. A particularly illuminating example is provided by *Piqua Branch of the State Bank of Ohio* v. *Knoop,* 16 Howard 369 (1854); for the full treatment of Ohio's promotional and regulatory efforts, see Ernest L. Bogart, *Internal Improvements and State Debt in Ohio* (New York: Longmans, Green & Company, Inc., 1924).

18. *Louisville, Cincinnati and Charleston Railroad* v. *Letson,* 2 Howard 478 (1844).

19. Felix Frankfurter and James M. Landis, *The Business of the*

Supreme Court (New York: The Macmillan Company, 1927), pp. 50–65.

20. Dissent in *Marshall* v. *Baltimore and Ohio Railroad,* 16 Howard 314 (1853).

21. Dissent in *Dodge* v. *Woolsey,* 18 Howard 331, 373 (1855).

22. Illustrative of this tendency were *Lochner* v. *New York* and *Coppage* v. *Kansas,* 195 U.S. 45 (1905) and 236 U.S. 1 (1915), respectively.

23. In fact, the political power wielded by rural America in modern times has frequently been influenced by nonagricultural groups usually oriented in behalf of corporate industry or organized labor; see especially Wesley McCune, *Who's behind Our Farm Policy?* (New York: Frederick A. Praeger, Inc., 1956), and Grant McConnell, *The Decline of Agrarian Democracy* (Berkeley: The University of California Press, 1953).

24. See, for example, Donald K. David *et al., The Little Economies: Problems of U.S. Area Development,* which compromises several papers delivered at the May 29, 1958, meeting of the Board of Trustees of the Committee for Economic Development (New York: Committee for Economic Development, 1958).

25. 206 U.S. 46 (1907).

26. Quoted in William Anderson *et al., The Nation and the States, Rivals or Partners?* (Minneapolis: University of Minnesota Press, 1955), p. 6.

27. Frank F. Fernbach, "Labor's Role in Political Affairs," a speech delivered before the Institute of Public Affairs, Charlottesville, Va., June 27, 1952.

28. All the public policy stands listed may be found in the annual publication of the proceedings of the House of Delegates in the *American Bar Association Journal,* 1937, through July, 1959.

29. Proceedings of the House of Delegates, *38 American Bar Association Journal* (1952), 428.

30. Frederick Bernays Wiener, Letter, *44 American Bar Association Journal* (1958), 1136–1138.

31. *39 American Bar Association Journal* (1953), 876.

32. Quoted in John J. Parker, "The Federal Judiciary," *24 American Bar Association Journal* (1938), 239–244.

33. John J. Parker, "The Federal Judiciary," *24 American Bar Association Journal* (1938), 239–244, 319–321.

34. Edward S. Corwin, "The Doctrine of Due Process of Law before the Civil War," *1 Selected Essays on Constitutional Law* (1930), 203–235; Wallace Mendelson, "Missing Link in the Evolution of Due Process," *10 Vanderbilt Law Review* (1956–1957), 125 ff.; Leonard W. Levy, *The Law of the Commonwealth and Chief Justice Shaw* (Cambridge, Mass.: Harvard University Press, 1957), pp. 109–117; and Monrad G. Paulsen, "Natural Rights—A Constitutional Doctrine in Indiana," *25 Indiana Law Journal* (1949–1950), 123–147.

35. For an intensive study of the changing social patterns of selection of members of, and candidates for, the Iowa Supreme Court, see Thomas A. Ewers, "A Study of the Backgrounds of the Successful and Unsuccessful Candidates for the Iowa Supreme Court, 1838–1958" (Unpublished Master's thesis, State University of Iowa, 1959); see also Timothy G. Higgins, "The Justices of the Wisconsin Supreme Court," *1949 Wisconsin Law Review,* pp. 738–760.

36. 348 U.S. 483 (1955). This broad statement is, of course, qualified elsewhere in the opinion. The statement deserves emphasis, however, for its symbolic importance.

37. Frank Hogan, "Important Shifts in Constitutional Doctrines," *25 American Bar Association Journal* (1939), 629–638.

38. Editorial, *25 American Bar Association Journal* (1939), 40.

39. Committee Report, *25 American Bar Association Journal* (1939), 658.

40. *Ibid.*

41. Editorial, *24 American Bar Association Journal* (1938), 373.

42. Walter P. Armstrong, "The Increasing Importance of State Supreme Courts," *28 American Bar Association Journal* (1942), 2–3; italics mine. Reprinted with the permission of the American Bar Association.

43. Of particular importance was the repudiation of *Swift* v. *Tyson,* 16 Peters 1 (1842), by the national Supreme Court; see *Erie Railroad* v. *Tompkins,* 304 U.S. 64 (1938).

44. See, especially, Monrad G. Paulsen, "The Persistence of Substantive Due Process in the States," *34 Minnesota Law Review* (1949–1950), 91–118; also Daniel J. Dykstra, "Legislative Favoritism before the Courts," *27 Indiana Law Journal* (1951–1952), 38–57; and John A. C. Hetherington, "State Economic Regulation and Substantive Due Process," *53 Northwestern University Law Review* (1958–1959), 13–32, 226–251.

45. Dykstra, *loc. cit.*

46. George W. Maxey, "The Equilibrium between Liberty and Government," *30 American Bar Association Journal* (1944), 66.

47. *Olsen* v. *Nebraska,* 313 U.S. 236 (1941).

48. *Boomer* v. *Olsen,* 143 Nebraska 579, 585–586, 10 N.W. 2nd 507, 511–515 (1943).

49. *State* v. *Harris,* 216 N.C. 746, 763, 6 S.W. 2nd 854 (1940).

50. *Moore* v. *Sutton,* 185 Va. 481, 490, 39 S.E. 348, 352 (1946).

51. Opinion of the Justices, 322 Mass. 755, 79 N.E. 2nd 883 (1948); for the materials cited in footnotes 47–51, cf. Paulsen, "Substantive Due Process."

52. Paulsen, "Substantive Due Process," pp. 116–117; in Paulsen's appraisal of the state courts through 1949, no state court had invalidated a state labor statute solely on state due process grounds.

53. *Iowa-Illinois Gas and Electric Company* v. *City of Fort Dodge,* 86 N.W. 2nd 28 (Iowa, 1957); Larson's decision was applied approvingly

in *Minneapolis Street Railway* v. *Minneapolis,* 86 N.W. 2nd 657 (Minnesota, 1957); and *Missouri ex rel. Missouri Water Company* v. *Public Service Commission,* 308 S.W. 2nd 704 (Missouri, 1957).

54. Fundamental changes in doctrinal attitudes have, of course, occurred. The Supreme Court of Michigan virtually revolutionized its doctrinal approach to workmen's compensation issues in the four-year period, 1954–1958, when five Mennen Williams Democrats acquired seats on the court; Glendon Schubert, *Quantitative Analysis of Judicial Behavior* (Glencoe, Ill.: The Free Press, 1960), pp. 129–142.

55. *Naim* v. *Naim,* 87 S.E. 2nd 749, 752, 756 (Virginia, 1955).

56. Monrad G. Paulsen, "State Constitutions, State Courts and First Amendment Freedoms," *4 Vanderbilt Law Review* (1950–1951), 620–642; and Walter Gellhorn (ed.), *The States and Subversion* (Ithaca, N.Y.: Cornell University Press, 1952).

57. Francis A. Allen, "The Supreme Court, Federalism, and State Systems of Criminal Justice," *8 University of Chicago Law School Record* [Special Supplement] (1958), 3–23.

58. Walter V. Schaefer, Associate Justice of the Illinois Supreme Court, *Courts and the Commonplaces of Federalism* (Champaign-Urbana, Ill.: Government Research Bureau, 1959), p. 18.

59. *Report of the Committee on Federal-State Relationships as Affected by Judicial Decisions of the Conference of State Chief Justices* (see note 6). "Report of the Special Committee on Habeas Corpus to the Conference of State Chief Justices," *26 State Government* (1953), 242–246, and Louis Pollack, "Proposals to Curtail Federal Habeas Corpus to State Prisoners," *66 Yale Law Journal* (1956–1957), 50–66.

60. 245 Iowa 147, 60 N.W. 2nd 110 (Iowa, 1954).

61. *Ibid.,* pp. 155–156.

62. Frank E. Holman, "Forms of Government," *32 American Bar Association Journal* (1946), 190; and Hatton W. Sumners, "The American Capacity for Self-Government Is Being Destroyed by Bureaucracy," *30 American Bar Association Journal* (1944), 5; while neither Holman nor Sumners wrote in an official capacity on these occasions, their views may be considered important in as much as both men were later recipients of the ABA Gold Medal for Conspicuous Service. Holman later was elected ABA President.

63. Joseph Henderson, "Making Secure the Blessings of Liberty," *30 American Bar Association Journal* (1944), 604.

64. All of the following are in *30 American Bar Association Journal* (1944): George Maxey, "The Equilibrium between Liberty and Government," p. 66; Hatton W. Sumners, "The American Capacity for Self-Government Is Being Destroyed by Bureaucracy," p. 3; Frank W. Grinnell, "The New Guesspotism," p. 507; and George Wharton Pepper, "The Need for Faith in the American System," p. 568.

65. *31 American Bar Association Journal* (1945), 573; Ben W. Palmer's

articles may be found in the following volumes: *32* (1946), 731; *34* (1948), 554, 677, 761, 887, 1000, 1092; *35* (1949), 12, 101, 189; for editorials recommending Palmer's articles, see volume *35* (1949), 129, 224.

66. *33 American Bar Association Journal* (1947), 150.

67. *Ibid.*, p. 585.

68. *Ibid.*, p. 110.

69. Editorial, *33 American Bar Association Journal* (1947), 4–5; see in same volume, Julian P. Alexander, "States of the Union: Time to Start Restoring Their Powers," pp. 3 ff., and Senator Pat McCarren, "Restoring Our Federal System," p. 52.

70. *34 American Bar Association Journal* (1948), 392.

71. *35 American Bar Association Journal* (1949), 566.

72. House of Delegates Proceedings, *44 American Bar Association Journal* (1958), 386–388.

73. In addition to the *ABA Journal* editorial criticisms indicated above, see ABA President Frank E. Holman's criticism of *Shelley* v. *Kraemer,* in his annual address entitled "Must America Succumb to Statism?" *35 American Bar Association Journal* (1949), 801 ff., or ABA President E. Smyth Gambrell's criticism of "the trend toward a political conception of the judicial power," in an address entitled "The American Faith and the Federal Judiciary," *42 American Bar Association Journal* (1950), 744.

74. See, for example, Edward J. Fox, Jr., "The Selection of Federal Judges: The Work of the Federal Judiciary Committee," *43 American Bar Association Journal* (1957), 685 ff.

75. For example, in 1953, ABA President William J. Jameson commented upon the very successful meeting of "three groups not directly affiliated with the House of Delegates but closely allied to the Association, i.e., the Conference of Chief Justices, the Conference of Bar Presidents and the American Law Student Association," *39 American Bar Association Journal* (1953), 859.

76. *45 American Bar Association Journal* (1959), 150.

77. It is not the purpose of this chapter to provide a point-by-point analysis of the Report of the Conference of Chief Justices. For appraisals challenging the accuracy of the charges made by this *Report,* see John D. O'Reilly, Jr., "The Spencer Roanes of 1958," *4 Villanova Law Review* (1958–1959), 92–116; and William B. Lockhart, "Response to the Conference of State Chief Justices," *107 University of Pennsylvania Law Review* (1958–1959), 802–810.

78. These appraisals may be found in *8 University of Chicago Law School Record* [Special Supplement] (1958); they consist of the following articles: Francis A. Allen, "The Supreme Court, Federalism, and State Systems of Criminal Justice," p. 3; Roger C. Cramton, "Limitations of State Power to Deal with Issues of Subversion and Loyalty," p. 24; Allison Dunham, "Congress, the States and Commerce," p. 54; Philip B. Kurland,

"The Supreme Court, the Due Process Clause, and the In Personam Jurisdiction of State Courts," p. 65; Bernard D. Meltzer, "The Supreme Court, the Congress, and State Jurisdiction over Labor Relations," p. 95; Allison Dunham, "The Role of the State Supreme Court in the Adjudication of Federal Questions," p. 140; Philip B. Kurland, "The Distribution of Judicial Power between National and State Courts," p. 145.

79. See especially Allen, *loc. cit.*, p. 18.

80. In the most recent appraisal three fourths of the state supreme courts so indulged, Heatherington, *loc. cit.*

81. *43 American Bar Association Journal* (1957), 1050.

—— *III*

The Significance for Judicial
Behavior of the Supreme Court's
Internal Procedures and Customs

5

The Evolution of the Supreme Court's
Internal Procedures and Customs

THE ASSESSMENT of the quality of judicial work and, inevitably, of the justices who produce such work would necessarily be incomplete if it were limited to consideration of the origin of the method of judicial selection, the social, ideological, and political realities incidental to the application of this selection method since 1789, and the private external influences brought to bear by ideologically motivated professional legal groups. These factors undoubtedly are of significance to the challenging study of judicial behavior, but the question remains, how significant? If judicial nominees for the nation's highest tribunal were merely products of their own social and ideological pasts or if they were measurably susceptible to external pressures, it would be a relatively easy task to formulate an answer. However, the newly appointed justice assumes or is expected to assume responsibility for maintaining the traditions of an institution generally quite unique to his experience. The internal procedures and traditions of the Supreme Court in themselves are factors which must be evaluated in the consideration of the roots of judicial behavior. What are the more significant internal procedures and traditions of the Supreme Court? Whence did they originate and what functions do they fulfill? What impact have these procedures and traditions had upon judicial behavior?

The decision-making process of the Supreme Court has customarily been treated as either the best of all possible procedural arrangements or as a professional mystery understood only by a privileged and small group of initiates. Neither of these treatments is calculated to broaden the layman's understanding of the internal operations of the Court. They tend to channel discussion of the Court's activities rather exclusively to analysis of *what* the Supreme Court has decided rather than to *how* the cases are decided. Because of lack of information, the problems attending the method of reaching decisions frequently must be ignored or dealt with on the basis of imagination and rumor rather than fact.

There are, of course, good and sufficient reasons why the current internal actions of the Supreme Court should remain secret. For example, the premature disclosure of the voting intentions of individual justices could irreparably damage public confidence in the Court and, because many decisions have important financial consequences outside the circle of litigants, give the recipients of such information an unfair advantage. However, objections of this sort need not be invoked to discourage or thwart investigations of internal procedural developments and problems if such investigations stop short of current litigation. A vast body of material is available in the many judicial biographies completed in the past three decades and in numerous but scattered law review articles.

The Evolutionary Nature of the Supreme Court's Internal Procedures and Customs

Although most discussions of judicial procedure treat the problem as one primarily concerned with the achievement of impartiality and efficiency,[1] there is a good deal of historical evidence which indicates that the evoluton of the Supreme Court's internal procedures and customs was strongly influenced by the currents and eddies of political conflict. Such matters as the customary attitudes toward the writing of dissenting and concurring opinions, the influential role of the Chief Justice, and the procedures for determining the jurisdictional competence of the Court all were conditioned, at least in part, by the political realities of eras long forgotten. This statement is not meant to discount the importance of considerations of the need for impartiality and efficiency but to point up the often close relation of these formal explanations for internal procedural change to informal but sometimes decisive political and ideological controversies.

The Formative Years

The institutional arrangements governing Supreme Court action during the first decade of its existence were conducive to individuality in decision making to a degree that has probably never been approximated since 1800. The practice of writing seriatim opinions which was adopted under the Chief Justiceship of John Jay and continued under John Rutledge and in modified form under Oliver Ellsworth left to the individual justices the greatest freedom in the presentation of their views. Even in the most important of the early Supreme Court decisions— *Chisholm* v. *Georgia, Hylton* v. *United States, Ware* v. *Hylton,* and *Calder* v. *Bull* [2]—the mode of internal decision making permitted the expression of shades and variations in reasoning, whether in concurrences or dissent, which has scarcely been equaled since.

It is of course true that in certain circumstances, such as the tenures of Chief Justices Roger B. Taney and Harlan Fiske Stone,[3] the members of the Supreme Court demonstrated a strong propensity for writing dissenting and concurring opinions. However, only in the formative decade did the internal procedures and customs of the Court encourage such judicial behavior. After 1800, variation in the expression of judicial reasoning and decision occurred largely in spite of the Court's procedures and traditions.

The practice of writing seriatim opinions was not the only indication of the relatively independent position of the individual justices prior to 1800. Justice Iredell's correspondence with Chief Justice Jay and Justices Cushing and Wilson reveals that the assignment of individual members to circuits was made by a majority of the justices rather than by the Chief Justice.[4] Furthermore, Chief

Justice Jay's correspondence indicates rather clearly that he considered the appointment of staff assistants to the Court a subject for group decision. For example, when Fisher Ames, apparently for patronage purposes, suggested that John Tucker of Massachusetts be appointed Clerk of the Supreme Court, Jay replied that such an appointment "should be the result of mutual information and joint consultation between the judges. . . ." [5] The practice of writing seriatim opinions was abandoned after the ascension of John Marshall to the Supreme Court. However, the other modes of internal operation considered above remained matters for group decision.

The immediate origin of the Supreme Court's procedures was in the era of John Jay and his early successors to the Chief Justiceship, John Rutledge and Oliver Ellsworth. The modes of internal operation adopted by Jay and his immediate successors did not, of course, determine the main characteristics of modern Court procedure and custom. In many respects, the first decade of the Supreme Court was a transitional one with respect to these matters. The sketchy biographical sources of this period suggest that Chief Justice Jay adapted to the needs of the Supreme Court the method of internal operation which was considered traditional in Great Britain but which had been temporarily abandoned during the tenure of Lord Mansfield.

Perhaps the clearest description of this development was given in a letter from Thomas Jefferson to Justice William Johnson in 1822. By that date the foundations for the modern methods of internal operation had been firmly established by Chief Justice John Marshall. Jefferson was severely critical of the newer modes of decision making and felt that traditional English and contemporary Virginia methods were more appropriate in a democratic society, a viewpoint which will be developed and analyzed fully later. To Johnson, he wrote,

> There is a subject respecting the practice of the court of which you are a member, which has long weighed on my mind. . . . The subject of my uneasiness is the habitual mode of making up and delivering the opinions of the supreme court of the U.S. You know that from the earliest ages of the English law, from

the date of the yearbooks, at least, to the end of the IId George, the judges of England, in all but self-evident cases, delivered their opinions seriatim, with the reasons and authorities which governed their decisions. If they sometimes consulted together, and gave a general opinion, it was so rarely as not to excite either alarm or notice. Besides the light which their separate arguments threw on the subject, and the instruction communicated by their several modes of reasoning, it shewed (sic) whether the judges were unanimous or divided, and gave accordingly more or less weight to the judgment as a precedent. It sometimes happened too that when there were three opinions against one, the reasoning of the one was so much the more cogent as to become afterwards the law of the land. When Ld. Mansfield came to the bench he introduced the habit of caucusing opinions. The judges met at their chambers, or elsewhere, secluded from the presence of the public, and made up what was to be delivered as the opinion the court. On the retirement of Mansfield, Ld. Kenyon put an end to the practice, and the judges returned to that of seriatim opinions, and practice it habitually to this day. . . . To come now to ourselves I know nothing of what is done in other states, but in this [Virginia] our great and good Mr. Pendleton was, after the revolution, placed at the head of the Court of Appeals. He adored Ld. Mansfield, and considered him as the greatest luminary of law that any age had ever produced, and he introduced into the court over which he presided, Mansfield's practice of making up opinions in secret and delivering them as the Oracles of the court, in mass. Judge Roane, when he came to that bench broke up the practice, refused to hatch judgments, in conclave, or to let others deliver opinions for him. At what time the seriatim opinions ceased in the Supreme Court of the U.S., I am not informed. They continued I know to the end of the 3d Dallas in in 1800. . . . About that time the present C.J. came to the bench. Whether he carried the practice of Mr. Pendleton to it, or who, or when I do not know; but I understand from others it is now the habit of the court. . . .[6]

It would probably be erroneous to assume that Jefferson's brief historical account fully explained the procedural changes which took place in the period 1789–1822, although his judgment concerning the historical origins of the modes of internal operations is accurate. The decision-making procedures to which Jefferson had referred were those utilized by the English Common Law Courts. Not only was the work of these courts familiar to America lawyers in this era,[7] but the mode of decision making developed by these English courts had been adopted by several of the courts of the states. Since a number of the early appointees of the United States, the most notable of which were John Blair and William Cushing,[8] had had colonial and state judicial experience before ascending the federal bench, it is probable that the adoption of the method of seriatim decision making in part was based upon the experiences of some of the colonial and state courts.[9] The adoption of the traditional mode by early members of the Supreme Court not only probably reflected close personal acquaintance with the method but was a manifestation of Chief Justice John Jay's deep-rooted caution when dealing with innovation, as well as a manifestation of the comparative absence of effective partisan political competition to the Federalist party.

The Marshall Era

When John Marshall became Chief Justice a rather complete reversal of internal procedural policy took place. This reversal had been harbingered to some extent under the Chief Justiceship of Oliver Ellsworth. During Ellsworth's tenure the Federalists had controlled all the branches of the national government. However, the Jeffersonian Republicans had shown considerable strength at the close of George Washington's second presidential term and became more aggressive during the stormy presidency of John Adams. Adams' presidency virtually coincided with the Chief Justiceship of Ellsworth. The justices of the Supreme Court, all Federalists, became increasingly involved in partisan controversy, particularly with respect to the enforcement in the circuit courts of the Alien and Sedition Acts, the attempt at establishing a common law jurisdiction for the federal courts, and the extremely partisan charges to grand juries made by several Court members while on circuit duty.[10] During much of this period there was a marked decline in the number of seriatim opinions, a symptom

perhaps of a growing conviction on the part of Chief Justice Ellsworth of the need for the Federalist justices to present a united
front to their political critics. The method of writing seriatim
opinions was not abandoned, however, until Marshall's ascension
to the supreme bench.[11]

The defeat of John Adams by Thomas Jefferson made imperative a greater degree of effectiveness by the Federalists, who
completely controlled the Supreme Court. The old Federalists
on the Court obviously had the determination to oppose Jeffersonian Republicanism and had demonstrated it for years on the
supreme bench and in numerous terms in the circuits. It remained
for John Marshall to combine such determination with procedural
innovations designed to facilitate efficient utilization of this Federalist domination of the Supreme Court. The longevity of the
aged and often ill Federalists on the Court aided this design. For
the first four years of Thomas Jefferson's presidency not a single
Supreme Court vacancy occurred. During this period, Marshall
established modes of internal procedure which irrevocably gave
the Chief Justice a key role in the decision-making process and
seriously reduced the independence of the individual justices in
this process.

For four crucial years, 1801–1804, the voice of the Supreme
Court was John Marshall's. Immediately, in the first decision handed
down under his Chief Justiceship, Marshall instituted the policy
not only of urging the Court to present a unified opinion but of
writing that opinion himself.[12] In this four-year period Marshall
wrote twenty-four of the twenty-six decisions containing opinions.
The two which he did not write involved cases coming from Marshall's circuit. Marshall felt it improper to participate in these.
This same period saw the disappearance of dissent from the Court
and, with one exception, the abandonment of the writing of concurring opinions.[13]

How did Marshall accomplish his objectives concerning the
Court's internal procedures? It has long been fashionable in academic circles to explain the developments in the early years of
Marshall's tenure as resulting from Marshall's dominance of his
older Federalist colleagues or from Marshall's winning social pres-

ence. However, it should be noted that Marshall's Federalist colleagues were men of considerable political and legal stature [14]
and, consequently, were not apt to accept any domineering by a
new member of the Court even if the novice were the Chief Justice.
Moreover, the tone of Marshall's correspondence with his fellow
Federalists suggests neither dominance nor mere social persuasion.
Marshall did, of course, attempt to develop cordial social relations,
but in dealing with the basic issues of Court policy in the face of
Jeffersonian control of the executive and legislative branches of
the national government, his approach to the other members of
the Court was businesslike and reserved. When, for example, the
Federalist justices considered the alternatives presented to them
by the Jeffersonian repeal of the Judiciary Act of 1801, Justice
Samuel Chase had argued that they should refuse to serve in the
circuit courts because the circuit judges created by the Act of 1801
had been unconstitutionally removed from office. Bushrod Washington had taken a contrary position, favoring compliance on the
ground that a precedent for circuit duty had already been set. Marshall himself played a relatively reserved role, polling the views
of the justices by mail and accepting as Supreme Court policy the
advice of the majority.[15] Incidents of this kind suggest that the
procedural innovations adopted after 1800 came as a result of the
unanimous choice of the Federalist justices in the face of the
changing conditions brought about by the sweeping Jeffersonian
political victory.

When William Johnson, the first Jeffersonian Republican on
the Court, was appointed in 1804, he described the situation in the
following terms:

> While I was on our state bench I was accustomed to delivering
> seriatim opinions in our appellate court, and was not a little sur-
> prised to find our Chief Justice in the Supreme Court delivering
> all the opinions in cases in which he sat, *even in some instances*
> *when contrary to his own judgment and vote.* But I remonstrated
> in vain; the answer was he was willing to take the trouble and
> it is a mark of respect for him. I soon however found out the real
> cause. Cushing was incompetent. Chase could not be got to think
> or write—Patterson (sic) was a slow man and willingly declined

the trouble, and the other two judges [Washington and Marshall] you know are commonly estimated as one judge.[16]

Johnson's explanation is lacking in one vital ingredient—serious motivation. The correspondence of Marshall and the other Federalist justices discussed above would indicate that common agreement rather than age and indolence provided the basis for internal developments within the Court.

The Interplay of Ideological Objective and Procedural Innovation

Chief Justice Marshall was, of course, adroit in the social arts and actively sought to create an atmosphere of social (and consequently, judicial) solidarity through two closely related techniques, the fostering of intimate social relations among the Supreme Court members and the conscious creation of habits and customs which were calculated to establish firmly the internal procedural setting which Marshall considered desirable. These techniques grew in importance after 1804 when death began to take a slow but steady toll of Federalist justices.

Marshall recognized clearly the value of social-group manipulation as a means of achieving not only unity in decision making but also ideological ascendancy. Many of his letters to Joseph Story reflect serious concern about seemingly petty trifles such as the choice of a boarding house commonly shared by the Court members. But, as a matter of fact, Marshall took such matters seriously because he felt that close social relations were essential to decision-making uniformity. In part this reflected the physical condition of some of the Court members,[17] but to a great extent it was an indication of Marshall's shrewd understanding of social manipulation. Marshall was an innovator, consciously setting group behavior patterns which reflected his own conception of the role of the Supreme Court in American politics and society. Since the Federalist justices during the early years of Marshall's tenure were generally in substantial agreement with him on procedural matters, the real test of Marshall's ability as a procedural innovator came after 1804. By the 1830's a majority of the Court was irrevocably Jeffersonian Republican in political background. Yet Marshall's conservative doctrines generally prevailed, and a good many of his procedural innovations became permanent parts of the internal arrangements of the Supreme Court.

Perhaps the letter of Marshall to Story, written on May 3, 1831, is one of the clearest indications of Marshall's awareness of the interplay of social setting and judicial unanimity. Marshall stated,

> I am apprehensive that the revolutionary spirit which displayed itself in our circle will, like most other revolutions, work inconvenience and mischief in its progress. I believe Mr. Brown does not count on boarding the Judges next winter; and if any other arrangement is made 'tis entirely unknown to me. We have, like most other unquiet men, discontented with the things that are, discarded accommodations which are reasonably convenient without providing a substitute. We pull down without inquiring how we are to build up. The matter rests I understand with our younger brother [Johnson], and he has probably committed it to some other person. If he had made an arrangement we should, I presume, have heard something about it. *I think this is a matter of some importance, for if the Judges scatter ad libitum, the docket, I fear, will remain quite compact, losing very few of its causes; and the few it may lose will probably be carried off by seriatim opinions.* Old men, however, are timid, and I hope my fears may be unfounded.[18]

It is clear that Marshall recognized that the principle of uniformity which he predicated as necessary to the effectiveness of the Supreme Court in preserving Federalist principles was a *sina qua non* of internal procedure. Uniformity, he realized, could be achieved, not by domination of the other members of the Court (some of whom, like William Johnson, were as strong-willed as Marshall himself), but as was noted above, through the social arts and by consciously creating habits and customs of proceeding which were calculated to establish firmly the procedural setting which Marshall considered desirable. Deviants from these norms of social and procedural behavior were subjected to strong social pressure. Justice William

Johnson had attempted to break Marshall's monopoly over decision making on several occasions. In the same letter to Jefferson in which he had discussed the ostensible reasons for Marshall's ascendancy, Johnson made the following revealing comments:

> Some case soon occurred in which I differed from my brethern, and I thought it a thing of course to deliver my opinion. But during the rest of the session I heard nothing but lectures on the indecency of judges cutting at each other, and the loss of reputation which the Virginia appellate court had sustained by pursuing such a course. At length I found that I must either submit to circumstances or become such a cypher in our consultations as to effect no good at all. I therefore bent to the current, and persevered until I got them to adopt the course they now pursue, which is to appoint someone to deliver the opinion of the majority, but leave it to the discretion of the rest of the judges to record their opinions or not ad libitum.[19]

The basic pattern that finally emerged as a result of Justice Johnson's efforts at breaking the opinion-writing monopoly of Chief Justice Marshall and at opening up free opportunities for the writing of dissenting or concurring opinions was not, of course, a return to the practices of the formative years of Jay, Rutledge, and Ellsworth. It was, rather, the establishment of a procedural compromise. The Chief Justice, when in the majority on a particular case, still dominated the case-assignment function, although he did not presume to write all the decisions himself. The writing of dissents and concurrences was only grudgingly conceded, and the members of the Court who engaged in the practice were subjected to strong social and moral pressures, for deviants were always accused of weakening the Court's authority and destroying its unity. Under Marshall this policy had the result of relegating dissent and, to a great extent, concurrence to matters not of doubt about the validity of a decision but of the strongest opposition. Marshall himself even wrote the Court's opinion in a case in which he personally disagreed with the stand he publicly espoused. He described his general personal practice in a comment in *Bank of the United States* v. *Dandridge:* [20]

I should now, as is my custom, when I have the misfortune to differ from this court, acquisce silently in its opinion, did I not believe that the judgment of the circuit court of Virginia [now affirmed by the majority] gave general surprise to the profession, and was generally condemned.

The price of maintaining the fiction of judicial certainty, decisiveness, and unity was the camouflaging of real doubt, and occasionally, the acceptance by individual justices of positions which they personally knew to be erroneous. Justice Story was, without doubt, the most careful legal scholar on the Supreme Court during this period. Yet he was persuaded, on several occasions, to accept erroneous decisions silently for the sake of the Court's reputation and unity. In a letter to his close personal friend, the Court Reporter Henry Wheaton, Justice Story described one such incident.

> At the earnest suggestion (I will not call it by a stronger name) of Mr. Justice Washington, I have determined not to deliver a dissenting opinion in *Olivera* v. *The United Insurance Company* (3 Wheaton's R. 183). The truth is, I was never more entirely satisfied that any decision was wrong, than that this is, but Judge Washington thinks (and very correctly) that the habit of delivering dissenting opinions on ordinary occasions weakened the authority of the Court, and is of no public benefit. It is no small proof of my good nature, that I have yielded in this instance, for since my return I have read pretty fully on the subject, and am more and more convinced that my original opinion was right.[21]

During Marshall's tenure only a justice of very strong convictions, notably William Johnson, broke the pattern of uniformity with consistency. With Marshall's death this procedural legacy was bestowed upon the Taney Court.

The Taney Court and Internal Procedure

Did the Taney Court accept the procedural legacy of the era of Marshall, or did it seriously attempt to alter the Supreme Court's internal arrangements? The biographical data indicate that while there were some changes in emphasis, the basic pattern of internal procedures evolved during the Marshall era was accepted and perpetuated by the Taney Court. In 1874 John A. Campbell described the broad outline of the Taney Court's internal operation in the following terms:

> The duties of the Justices of the Supreme Court consist in the hearing of cases; the preparations for the consultations; the consultations in the conference of the judges; the decision of the cause there, and the preparation of the opinion and the judgment of the court. Their most arduous and responsible duty is in the conference. . . .
>   . . . The Chief Justice presided, the deliberations were usually frank and candid. . . .
>   In these conferences, the Chief Justice usually called the case. He stated the pleadings and facts that they presented, the arguments and his conclusions in regard to them, and invited discussion. The discussion was free and open among the justices till all were satisfied.
>   The question was put, whether judgment or decree should be reversed, and each justice, according to his precedance, commencing with the junior judge, was required to give his judgment and his reasons for his conclusion. The concurring opinions of the majority decided the cause and signified the matter of the opinion to be given. The Chief Justice designated the judge to prepare it.[22]

Taney, in his own way, made himself as fully a master of the internal procedures of the Court as his predecessor. The procedural arrangements inherited from Marshall undoubtedly provided Taney as many opportunities for the development of a body of Jacksonian Democratic doctrines as they had afforded Marshall the chance to reiterate Federalist principles. Thus radical change was probably deemed unnecessary. In addition, the Court's work load became, during Taney's tenure, a problem of compelling importance.[23] A return to the practice of writing seriatim opinions, even if it had been desired, would have been a practical impossibility.

Taney to some extent permitted—on some occasions could not prevent—the writing of separate opinions in areas such as the interpretation of the commerce clause, where the Court was sharply divided. By the late 1840's, it became apparent that the increasing caseload was making heavy demands on the justices. Reverdy Johnson, an outstanding lawyer of the period, described the working habits of the Court in 1848.

> They meet at eleven o'clock and hear arguments until four. Then they retire to their rooms; dine at five; go into consultation almost every day at seven; sit until nine, ten, eleven, or twelve at night. In the morning generally, their opinions are prepared, books have to be examined, records are to be pored over.[24]

Presumably, Taney might have utilized this situation to suggest a return to the policy of the early years of Marshall's Chief Justiceship. Instead of interfering with the modified freedom of dissent and concurrence, however, the Court preferred to limit drastically oral argument.[25] Despite the fact that Charles Warren's historical account of the golden age of unrestricted oratory is often restated, nostalgically, by modern commentators, there is little doubt that the preservation of the freedom of the conference was of far greater import than the long-winded histrionics of the colorful members of the Supreme Court's bar.

Despite some doctrinal differences between the Jacksonian appointees and the survivors of the Marshall era, the tradition of cordial personal relations was maintained and consciously cultivated by Chief Justice Taney. Justice Story, whose long tenure bridged many years of Marshall's service and many of Taney's, gave a number of insightful comments on these matters in his private letters. In one instance he commented, somewhat dismally, "The Supreme Court now consists of nine Judges, two having been lately added by an act of Congress. Mr. Taney is Chief Justice. I am the last of the old race of Judges. I stand their solitary representative, with a pained heart, and a subdued confidence." [26] Yet in another letter written in the same period, Story gave this favorable account of the Court's personal relations, "The Judges go on quite harmoniously. The new Chief Justice conducts himself with great urbanity and propriety. Judge Barbour is a very conscientious and painstaking Judge, and I think will improve as he goes on" [27]

The enlargement of the Supreme Court's membership had,

in the opinion of Story, its less attractive consequences. Writing to Sumner, March 15, 1838, Story commented,

> You may ask how the Judges got along together? We made very slow progress, and did less in the same time than I ever knew. The addition to our numbers has most sensibly affected our facility as well as the rapidity of doing business. "Many men of many minds" require a great deal of discussion to compel them to come to definite results; and we found ourselves often involved in long and very tedious debates. I verily believe, if there were twelve judges, we should do no business at all, or at least very little. So far as my personal comfort and personal intercourse were concerned, everything went on well.[28]

Although Story attributed the tendency toward tedious debate to the addition of new justices, this development may be recognized also as indicative of Taney's attitude toward the deliberative process and of the deep ideological differences that divided the Court during much of Taney's tenure as Chief Justice.

As the era of Jacksonian Democratic ascendancy neared its tragic end, the ideological differences became so deep that the tradition of gracious personal relations among Supreme Court members was seriously strained. A bitter exchange of letters between Chief Justice Taney and Associate Justice Curtis reflected the former's belief that an antislavery justice had leaked information regarding the Dred Scott case to James S. Pike, a reporter for the *New York Tribune*.[29] Conversely, Justice Curtis, in a letter to a relative completed shortly before his resignation from the Court, had written,

> I cannot feel that confidence in the Court, and that willingness to cooperate with them, which are essential to the satisfactory discharge of my duties as a member of that body; and I do not expect its condition to be improved.[30]

Despite the servere strains imposed by the fundamental ideological cleavages of the 1850's and of the Civil War itself, Chief Justice Taney managed through tact and courtesy to maintain a remarkable degree of comradeship and good will among Supreme

Court members. He thus succeeded in retaining intact the Court's manner of operation through the delicate years when President Lincoln was selecting a Republican majority for the Supreme Court.[31] Consequently, the Supreme Court emerged from the crucial transition period at the close of the Taney era with its mode of internal operation and its basic customs virtually unchanged.

The Post-Civil War Era and the Age of Reform

Perhaps the most important developments affecting the evolution of the internal procedures and customs of the Supreme Court were those great economic and social changes in America which were transforming the whole society. The growth of corporate industrial power—political and social as well as economic—accelerated in the post-Civil War decades. Corporate litigants preferred the more sympathetic federal courts to the occasionally hostile state court systems.[32] The general corporate desire to avoid the state judicial systems had as its concommitant the strong nationalistic attitude of congressional leaders in the immediate post-Civil War period.

The Taney Court had, of course, begun the process of opening the jurisdictional floodgates to corporate litigants in its ruling in the Letson case in 1844.[33] But the full sweep of corporation pressures in litigation before the federal courts was not felt until after the Civil War. Frankfurter and Landis recorded the build-up of cases pending before the Supreme Court as follows: 1850—253 cases; 1860—310 cases; 1870—636 cases; 1880—1,212; 1890—1,816 cases.[34] While the Letson doctrine of corporate citizenship increased the Supreme Court's diversity of citizenship jurisdiction, the post-Civil War congressional actions broadened the scope of federal judicial authority to encompass virtually every claimed federal right.[35] These post-Civil War acts marked a new era for the federal court system. Yet in terms of the internal working arrangements of the Supreme Court, the mode of operation inherited from a more leisurely era was retained.[36] Relief from the tremendous combination of work loads inherent in a system requiring both circuit riding [37] and an increasingly heavy appellate term in Washington was to come ultimately from Congress in 1891.[38]

While the major characteristics of the Court's method of internal operation were unchanged, the inauguration of the practice of employing a legal secretary or clerk by Justice Horace Gray [39] did represent an internal innovation which when universally adopted by the justices tended to lighten their individual burdens. One of Gray's selections to such a post, Samuel Williston, uniquely exemplified the characteristics of many of the young men who later held similar short appointments—he was an outstanding graduate of the law school which had produced the justice who selected him, was possessed of high intelligence, and was sufficiently independent and mature to challenge, albeit usually unsuccessfully, the positions of his superior on occasions where clerk and justice differed.[40]

The post-Civil War Era also brought with it a gradual stiffening of judicial attitudes toward the relations of Court members to either political party organizations or private interest groups. While it had generally been recognized that issues before the Court (or those likely to be brought before it) should not be discussed outside the confines of the Court's membership, there had been several occasions when Court members had not adhered to this tradition. For example, Justice William Johnson had submitted what was in effect an advisory opinion to President Monroe on the constitutionality of Congressional power to undertake and operate a variety of internal improvements.[41] Perhaps the most serious of the violations of the judicial proprieties occurred in connection with the Dred Scott case when Justice Catron disclosed to President Buchanan the alignment of the Court with respect to the pending decision. Buchanan used this information in his Inaugural Address.[42]

Those who erred for party prior to the Civil War were replaced by those who erred for interest group after that war. The efforts of corporation executives, particularly those of the railroads, to secure Court actions favorable to their interests were unceasing in the post-Civil War era. For men on the Court like Justice Samuel Freeman Miller, the increasing scope of influence of the railroad magnates was the occasion for deep private concern. As he expressed it to his brother-in-law, Ballinger,

> Certain members of the Supreme Court are *always* in favor of enforcing [railroad] bonds [in receivership cases], at the expense of all other rights. The men you are fighting have personal access to certain judges, whose influence on the bench is predominant. They understand beyond all men I have ever known the *art* of influencing men.[43]

Justice Field's associations with Leland Stanford,[44] and the law careers of Justices Bradley and Strong as advocates of railroad corporations [45] had aroused public criticism of the Supreme Court at the very time that a great many legal issues involving the railroads were being considered by the Court. The fact that Field conferred with railroad magnates with respect to issues pending in the *Sinking Fund Cases* [46] indicated that in at least one instance the judicial proprieties were strained if not violated. Two letters of railroad executive David D. Colton to Huntington in 1878 contained the following references. (August 9, 1878) "I have had several long talks with Judge Field and the hope of the country is in the Supreme Court if the nation is to be saved from disgrace." (September 20, 1878) "Judge Field will not sit in the Gallatin Case, but will reserve himself for his best efforts (I have no doubt) on the final determination of the case at Washington before a full bench." [47]

The realization that the reputation of the Supreme Court itself for impartiality might be endangered by such relations had led Chief Justice Waite to reprimand Field, in effect, in a letter exchange concerning the assignment of decision-writing chores. In response to a note from Field, Waite had written,

> We cannot conceal from ourselves the fact that in the excited state of feeling, which exists or has existed, with the public in respect to the connection of the government with the Union Pacific, there may be some feeling of disappointment at the result of this case. It seemed to me, therefore, to be especially important that the opinion should come from one who had not only been understood to be watchful of the government purse, but who

would not be known as the personal friend of the parties representing these railroad interests. There is no doubt of your intimate
personal relations with the managers of the Central Pacific, and
naturally you, more than anyone else, in the Court, realize the
vast importance of the great work that has been done. To tell you
the truth also, I knew that you were dissatisfied with the manner
of the argument on the part of the government and was afraid
that this might unconsciously to you find expression in your
opinion. . . .[48]

In a number of respects the Supreme Court developed its own
reflexes to such problems and, in particular, the respective Chief
Justices assumed a strong sense of responsibility for maintaining
and fostering the judicial proprieties. For example, Chief Justices
Waite and Fuller exercised careful discretion in the assignment of
opinion-writing chores. Fuller, especially, consciously sought to
avoid excessive participation in the social life of Washington and
is credited with starting a trend which left the members of the
Court in relative social isolation. Although Fuller's biographer
attributes this to a desire to avoid excessive eating,[49] Fuller's social
policy may well have indicated a desire to remove the possibility
that through intimate social relations with powerful interest group
representatives the Court members would appear to be in a posture
susceptible to improper or undue external influence. It should be
noted, however, that with the advent of the proposed legislation
designed to lighten the work load of the Court, Chief Justice Fuller
assiduously cultivated the key members of the Senate Judiciary
Committee.

The development of more cautious personal habits in the
social behavior of the justices was, of course, a factor which had
little impact upon the internal working patterns of the Court. Here
the significant events were the great transformations wrought by
congressional legislation, most notably the Judiciary Acts of 1891
and 1925. In addition, the operation of the Supreme Court was influenced considerably by the changing tempo and emphases of
American society. As Frankfurter and Landis so perceptively
pointed out, "no matter what the structure of the courts or the distribution of the judicial power, the business of the courts is deter-

mined by the nature and extent of the predominant activities of contemporary life." [50]

The essential contributions of the Judiciary Act of 1891 were threefold. Intermediate courts of appeals were set up, the jurisdiction of the federal courts redistributed in a manner designed to channel (in some instances directly) only the more important categories of cases to the Supreme Court, and compulsory attendance by the Supreme Court Justices on circuit duty was for all practical purposes ended.[51] The result of the enactment of this legislation was a considerable easing of the work load of the Supreme Court. However, within a relatively short span of years the caseload became a problem once again, this time as a result of the proliferation of economic issues coming before the Court.[52] Consequently, it was not until the enactment of the so-called "Judges' Bill" of 1925 that the Supreme Court itself was granted discretionary authority to grant or deny certiorari in virtually every major appellate field. In a few strictly limited areas review remained a matter of right. In practice, the distinction between the right of appeal and the discretionary grant of certiorari became a meaningless one.[53]

Chief Justice Taft, who played a vital role in drafting and securing passage for the Act, stated its essential philosophy in these terms:

> The sound theory of . . . the new act is that litigants have their rights sufficiently protected by a hearing or trial in the courts of first instance, and by one review in an intermediate appellate federal court. The function of the Supreme Court is conceived to be, not the remedying of a particular litigant's wrong, but the consideration of cases whose decision involves principles, the application of which are of wide public or governmental interest. . . .[54]

The congressional enactments of 1891 and 1925 permitted the Supreme Court to retain its institutional characteristics by lightening the work load of the justices in a variety of ways.

What is frequently overlooked is that the congressional contribution to the maintenance of the Court's internal procedures and customs was not limited to positive enactments but reflected, in as great a measure, an unwillingness to adopt proposals which would have inexorably altered the character of the Court as a consultative and deliberative body. After the Civil War a number of serious attempts were made to increase permanently the membership of the Supreme Court, to add temporary members, and to have the Court decide cases sitting in divisions. The consistent rejection of these proposals by Congress ensured the institutional integrity of the nineteenth-century Court. Yet the social imperatives of the twentieth century, in turn, demanded new internal procedural adjustments. The tremendous outpouring of social enactments during the 1930's brought in its wake not only the dramatic constitutional tests of this legislation but also the multitude of statutory interpretations. The tasks of statutory interpretation, though less likely to engage public attention, became of primary consequence especially after 1937.

Of equal importance was the growing concern of the Supreme Court for human nonproperty rights. This was reflected not only in the changing character of the issues coming to the Court but also by the assumption of the special burden of *in forma pauperis* petitions by Chief Justice Hughes and his successors. These petitions were usually from prison inmates who wrote or typed out the petitions themselves in the hope that an allegedly unfair conviction would be reversed. When Harlan Fiske Stone became Chief Justice in 1941 the number of such petitions totaled 178 annually. Stone described the development of responsibility by Chief Justices as follows:

> When I first came on the court [in 1925] *in forma pauperis* cases were treated rather lightly, but during Chief Justice Hughes' time and my own, we have examined them with great care. They are mostly chaff, but occasionally we find some grains of wheat in the chaff and those cases we assign counsel, pay expenses of printing the papers and hear the case. This has occasionally resulted in unearthing grave abuses in trial courts which deprived the petitioner of his constitutional rights.[55]

Viewed from an humanitarian aspect, the assumption of this burden by Hughes and his successors was a significant social advance; but viewed from the posture of cold-blooded administrative efficiency, the burden represented yet another addition to the already heavy work load of the Chief Justice. Since the Chief Justiceship of William Howard Taft, the Chief Justice has had increasing responsibility for providing administrative leadership for the entire regular federal court system. The duties and obligations related to the Judicial Conference were to find their counterpart in the expansion of the functions of the Administrative Office of the United States Courts. In both areas the Chief Justice had primary responsibility. As Stone put it,

> Few are aware that neither my predecessor, nor I in more than twenty years since I have been a Justice of the Supreme Court, have been able to meet the daily demands upon us without working night and holidays and Sunday. The administrative duties of the Chief Justice have increased, and many other duties have been imposed on him by acts of Congress which my predecessors were not called on to perform. . . . Unlike the functions of an executive officer, practically none of these can be delegated.[56]

Stone's successor to the Chief Justiceship, Fred M. Vinson, sought to ease the administrative pressures by appointing an administrative assistant to stand between the Chief Justice and the Administrative Office of the United States Courts, the Clerk of the Supreme Court, and the Court's Marshal, Reporter, and Librarian. Vinson also appointed two messengers (instead of one), and three law clerks (instead of two).[57]

Fundamentally, the most important problems besetting the modern chief justice are not those arising from the increasing administrative work load, although this factor cannot be ignored. Of overriding consideration are the problems of intracourt leadership which sensitively touch upon the ideological content of contemporary decision making and upon the modern Court's tendency for fullsome expression of dissenting and concurring opinions. Appraisal and evaluation of these problems in the context of modern American society are the primary purposes of the subsequent chapter.

References

1. For an example of this sort of apolitical treatment, see William Franklin Willoughby, *Principles of Judicial Administration* (Washington: The Brookings Institution, 1929).

2. 2 Dallas 419 (1793); 3 Dallas 171 (1796); 3 Dallas 199 (1797); and 3 Dallas 386 (1798), respectively.

3. See Carl B. Swisher, *Roger B. Taney* (New York: The Macmillan Company, 1935), pp. 393–411; and Alpheus T. Mason, *Harlan Fiske Stone: Pillar of the Law* (New York: The Viking Press, 1956), pp. 563–646.

4. Iredell felt that the action permanently assigning justices to particular circuits was manifestly unfair to the Southerners whose circuit was by far the largest in that period, Griffith J. McRee (ed.), *Life and Correspondence of James Iredell*, II (Gloucester, Mass.: Peter Smith, 1949), 320–325.

5. Henry P. Johnston (ed.), *Correspondence of John Jay*, III (New York: G. P. Putnam's Sons, 1890), 379.

6. Paul Leicester Ford (ed.), *Writings of Thomas Jefferson*, X (New York: G. P. Putnam's Sons, 1899), 223–224.

7. Karl M. ZoBell, "Division of Opinion in the Supreme Court: A History of Judicial Disintegration," *44 Cornell Law Quarterly* (1959), 190–191.

8. On Blair, see *Dictionary of American Biography*, II, 337–338; on Cushing, *Dictionary of American Biography*, IV, 633–635, and note, "William Cushing's Judicial Career in Massachusetts from 1777–1789," *48 Massachusetts Law Quarterly* (1958), 64–69.

9. See, for example, Jefferson's comments about the Virginia Supreme Court of Appeals, pp. 106–107; and Justice William Johnson's comments about the highest appellate court of South Carolina, p. 110; but ZoBell, drawing upon Pound, argues that the experience of the colonial courts was of little significance, *loc. cit.*, p. 191.

10. Charles Warren, *The Supreme Court in United States History*, II (Boston: Little, Brown & Company, 1922), 124–168.

11. Donald G. Morgan, *Justice William Johnson: The First Dissenter* (Columbia: University of South Carolina Press, 1954), pp. 46–47.

12. *Talbot* v. *Seeman*, 1 Cranch 1 (1801).

13. Justice Samuel Chase did write a concurring opinion in *Head* v. *Providence Insurance Company*, 2 Cranch 127 (1804).

14. See, for example, F. William O'Brien, "The Pre-Marshall Court and the Role of William Cushing," *48 Massachusetts Law Quarterly* (1958), 52–64.

15. Gertrude Sceery Wood, *William Paterson of New Jersey* (The author, 433 Van Houten St., Paterson, N.J., 1933), pp. 176–182.

16. Morgan, *op. cit.*, pp. 181–182.

17. Charles Warren, "Story-Marshall Correspondence, 1819–1831," *William and Mary College Quarterly Historical Magazine*, XXI (2nd Series, 1941), 24.

18. *Ibid.*, pp. 22–23; italics mine.

19. Johnson to Jefferson, December 10, 1822; quoted in Morgan, *op. cit.*, p. 182.

20. 25 U.S. 64, 90 (1827).

21. William Story (ed.), *The Life and Letters of Joseph Story*, II (Boston: Charles C. Little and James Brown, 1851), 303–304; for another example, see Story's reference to *U.S. v. Bevans*, p. 305.

22. From an address given by Campbell in honor of the late Benjamin Curtis, 87 U.S. x (1874).

23. The number of cases docketed grew from 92 in 1840 to 253 in 1850 and 310 in 1860, Felix Frankfurter and James M. Landis, *The Business of the Supreme Court* (New York: The Macmillan Company, 1927), p. 52, note 173.

24. Quoted in Alexander A. Lawrence, *James Moore Wayne, Southern Unionist* (Chapel Hill: University of North Carolina Press, 1943), p. 133.

25. Alfred Conkling, *Treatise on the Courts of the United States* (Albany, N.Y.: W. C. Little & Company, 1856), p. 780.

26. Story, *op. cit.*, II, 277.

27. *Ibid.*, p. 266.

28. *Ibid.*, p. 296.

29. Swisher, *Taney*, pp. 488–489; and Benjamin R. Curtis, *Life and Writings of Benjamin Robbin Curtis*, I (Boston: Little, Brown & Company, 1879), 211–248.

30. Letter to Tichnor, July 3, 1857, reproduced in Curtis, *op. cit.*, pp. 247–248.

31. For an excellent account of this crucial transition period, see David M. Silver, *Lincoln's Supreme Court* (Urbana: University of Illinois Press, 1956), pp. 94–103.

32. See, for example, Charles Fairman, *Mr. Justice Miller* (Cambridge, Mass.: Harvard University Press, 1939), pp. 207–249; Frankfurter and Landis, *op. cit.*, pp. 64–85.

33. *Louisville, Cincinnati and Charlestown Railroad v. Letson*, 2 Howard 478 (1844).

34. Frankfurter and Landis, *op. cit.*, p. 60.

35. *Ibid.*, pp. 64–85.

36. See, for example, Hoar's description of the post-Civil War operations of the Supreme Court contained in Charles Bradley (ed.), *Miscellaneous Writings of Joseph P. Bradley* (Newark, N.J.: L. J. Hardham, 1901), pp. 51, 71–74.

37. For an account of the nature of the circuit duties of the justices during the post-Civil War era, see Fairman, *op. cit.*, pp. 401–424.

38. Frankfurter and Landis, *op. cit.,* pp. 97–102.

39. Willard L. King, *Melville Weston Fuller* (New York: The Macmillan Company, 1950), p. 133.

40. Samuel Williston, *Law and Life* (Boston: Little, Brown & Company, 1941), pp. 86–101.

41. Morgan, *op. cit.,* pp. 122–124.

42. Swisher, *Taney,* pp. 495–502.

43. Fairman, *op. cit.,* p. 241.

44. Carl Brent Swisher, *Stephen J. Field, Craftsman of the Law* (Washington: The Brookings Institution, 1930), pp. 243–244.

45. J. W. Schuckers, *The Life and Public Services of Salmon Portland Chase* (New York: D. Appleton and Company, 1874), pp. 258–261.

46. 99 U.S. 700 (1879).

47. Swisher, *Field,* pp. 246–247.

48. Letter of November 10, 1875, quoted in Bruce R. Trimble, *Chief Justice Waite, Defender of the Public Interest* (Princeton, N.J.: Princeton University Press, 1938), pp. 261–262.

49. Willard L. King, *Melville W. Fuller* (New York: The Macmillan Company, 1950), pp. 153–154.

50. Frankfurter and Landis, *op. cit.,* p. 103.

51. *Ibid.,* pp. 86–102.

52. *Ibid.,* pp. 103–107.

53. Note, "The Insubstantial Federal Question," *62 Harvard Law Review* (1949), 488.

54. Alpheus T. Mason, *op. cit.,* p. 213.

55. *Ibid.,* p. 639.

56. Letter to President Truman, Feb. 13, 1946, *ibid.,* p. 719.

57. *Ibid.,* note 1.

_____ 6

A Contemporary Appraisal of the Institutional Procedures and Customs of the Supreme Court

IN THE post-World War II era, the internal procedures and customs of the Supreme Court have themselves become targets for ideological criticism. Such criticism has come from a variety of sources, including the radical right, some professional lawyers' groups, and civil libertarians. Consequently, any realistic appraisal of these institutional methods of operation must of necessity include some analysis not only of the conditions external to the Court that make for these criticisms but also of the internal institutional factors that are the primary subjects for analysis.

The Sifting Process

Perhaps the most striking attribute of the modern Supreme Court is its ability to control, to a great extent, both the volume and substance of the litigation which comes before it. Ultimately, the source of the Court's discretionary authority in most of its appellate jurisdiction is, of course, Congress and the Judiciary Act of 1925. The legislative substitution of the discretionary writ of certiorari for the obligatory writ of error was the key to a decisive change in the functioning of the Court. However, what is sometimes overlooked is the fact that all litigation submitted to the Supreme Court is sifted carefully before it is placed on the calendar for argument.

128

Whether a case comes to the Supreme Court in a petition for a writ of certiorari or on appeal, or whether it comes in the infrequent actions under the Court's original jurisdiction, or through invocation of one of the extraordinary writs (habeas corpus, prohibition, mandamus, and common law certiorari), or through certificate from a Court of Appeals or the Court of Claims, a preliminary examination of the case is made by the Supreme Court to determine whether the issue deserves full consideration.[1] Because approximately 87 per cent of the annual petitions or applications for review or relief are usually denied,[2] the sifting process may be considered of crucial importance.

The bestowal of discretionary authority upon the Supreme Court by Congress actually antedated the Judges' Bill of 1925. As early as 1891, discretionary power to scrutinize, in terms of their public importance, cases in limited areas was authorized in the Circuit Court of Appeals Act. In order to ensure that the exercise of such discretion did not become (or seem to become) the arbitrary choice of the justices, a procedural rule was soon developed under which the Court considered a case if four of the justices believed that the issues raised by it were of sufficient importance to warrant such action. The "rule of four" did not attract public attention until it was discussed fully during the Senate Judiciary Committee Hearings in 1924 which preceded the passage of the Judiciary Act of 1925. As is indicated above, this Act extended appreciably the discretionary authority of the Supreme Court.[3] Since 1925 the process by which the Supreme Court gives preliminary attention to cases brought before it has been the center of a number of controversies.

Most of the issues coming to the Supreme Court for possible consideration are submitted under the discretionary certiorari procedure or on appeal. While action on appeal is statutorily obligatory, the Court's treatment of such action resembles, in many respects, its summary treatment of petitions for writ of certiorari. Supreme Court Clerk Harold B. Willey wrote in this vein in 1945:

> Most attorneys are well aware of the fact that the Court may and does exercise its discretion in passing on applications for certiorari but insofar as appeals are concerned they harbor the mistaken im-

pression that review is obligatory and that where they have an appeal "as of right" they are entitled to oral argument on the merits. On the contrary, at least fifty per cent of the appeals are dismissed or the judgments affirmed upon consideration of the jurisdictional statements, before the records are printed and without oral argument. Jurisdictional statements and petitions for certiorari now stand on practically the same footing, and upon the case made in the former, just as in the latter, may depend the grant of further hearing.[4]

From the point of view of the Court, this development is incidental to its primary objective of reserving its efforts for the truly important legal issues. From the point of view of contemporary critics of the Court, the *de facto* extension of discretionary authority is held a violation of Congressional intent.

Although matters of this sort have been subjects for debate, the aspect of the Supreme Court's preliminary consideration of issues which has aroused the strongest criticism has been the administration of certiorari petitions. Civil libertarians, such as Fowler V. Harper, have deplored the fact that the Court has frequently refrained from considering issues which have far-reaching implications for the social and political evolution of a free society.[5] Denial of certiorari in the cases which Harper has dramatized [6] does not, of course, imply complete loss of opportunity to obtain the Court's consideration of such issues on their merits. Justice Frankfurter has pointed out on a number of occasions that reasons for a denial "of certiorari in the ordinary run of cases can be any number of things *other than* a decision on the merits." [7] Presumably, determined litigants who were convinced of the importance of their cases might try again via petition for rehearing or devise a new approach to the problem of persuading the Court of the significance of their cases.

However, in recent years, Frankfurter's contention has been challenged not only by critical law professors but by several members of the Court itself. Justice Jackson observed,

> Perhaps the profession could accept denial as meaningless before the custom was introduced of noting dissents from them.

Lawyers and lower judges will not readily believe that Justices of this Court are taking the trouble to signal a meaningless division of opinion about a meaningless act.[8]

The accuracy of Jackson's observation may be attested by the fact that the Department of Justice, the most frequent litigant before the Supreme Court, now usually submits briefs on the merits of each case [9] despite the fact that preliminary consideration of certiorari petitions is purportedly limited to assessment of the public importance of the issue or whether a conflict in judicial interpretation in the lower courts is present.[10] Clearly, the denial of certiorari has immediate consequences for the litigants, and, whether validly or not, such denial is viewed, on occasion, as settling the particular public policy issues raised.

In a somewhat different vein, Harper and Leibowitz have argued that the standards by which the justices apply their discretionary authority are too vague. Members of the legal profession, confronted by a situation in which most petitions for writ of certiorari are dealt with cryptically in *per curiam* opinions stating "certiorari granted" or "certiorari denied," have often increased rather than abandoned their efforts to obtain full consideration of their cases. Harper and Leibowitz concluded that this development has not simply confused lawyers but has made more difficult the Court's own task of speedily selecting from an annual assortment of hundreds of requests for consideration of legal issues only cases which are of great public significance. As the number of requests, whether in the form of petitions for writ of certiorari or jurisdictional statements invoking the right of appeal, tend to increase in number, the Court's margin of error in sifting the wheat from the chaff is apt to increase.[11] Errors resulting from overgenerous bestowal of the Court's consideration of issues may be, and often are, corrected by recourse to dismissal of a writ, after hearing, as "improvidently granted." However, errors resulting from parsimonious denial may not be rectified so easily. For example, petitions for rehearing of orders denying certiorari may be filed, but such actions are rarely successful.[12]

Members of the Supreme Court have often pointed out that

the Court's role in American society precluded mere correction of the errors of lower courts. Addressing the American Bar Association in 1949, Chief Justice Vinson pointed out:

> The function of the Supreme Court is . . . to resolve conflicts of opinion on federal questions that have arisen among lower courts, to pass upon questions of wide import under the Constitution, laws, and treaties of the United States, and to exercise supervisory power over lower federal courts. If we took every case in which an interesting legal question is raised, or our *prima facie* impression is that the decision below is erroneous, we could not fulfill the Constitutional and statutory responsibilities placed upon the Court. To remain effective, the Supreme Court must continue to decide only those cases which present questions whose resolution will have immediate importance far beyond the particular facts and parties involved. Those of you whose petitions for certiorari are granted by the Supreme Court will know, therefore, that you are, in a sense, prosecuting or defending class actions; that you represent not only your clients, but tremendously important principles, upon which are based the plans, hopes, and aspirations of a great many people throughout the country.[13]

Whether one argues, as has Ernest J. Brown, that the Supreme Court, despite its protestations, has acted on occasion as a "Court of Selected Error," [14] it is clear that the broad exercise of discretionary power to weed out the unimportant cases is the crucial stage for most federal litigation. Some members of the Court, notably Justice Frankfurter, have stressed the importance of the sifting process to the maintenance of the operating efficiency of the Court as a national institution. Frankfurter, in discussing and defending the propriety of dismissal of petitions for certiorari as "improvidently granted" after four justices had voted for consideration of the cases, invoked the argument that the majority must ultimately decide. In his words,

> The Court operates . . . by majority. Even though a minority may bring a case here for oral argument, that does not mean that the majority has given up its right to vote on the ultimate disposition of the case as conscience merits.[15]

The justification for particular procedural arrangements must rest upon the logical relation of such arrangements to the purposes for which the Court itself functions. Despite the increasing emphasis upon deciding only the important issues, it must be remembered that the Supreme Court is still a court of justice and that justice has traditionally been associated with such concepts as fair procedural arrangements and intelligible standards. Insofar as the criticisms of Harper and Brown have validity, the Court's summary treatment of certiorari petitions leaves a great deal to be desired. Not only are the standards for acceptance or denial ambiguous, but the Court's insistence, embodied in Rule 19, that it is interested in only the truly important cases, is misleading. Students of the Court have long understood that in many instances the Court seeks to avoid some important issues either by deliberately leaving their resolution to Congress or the President or by invocation of one of a multitude of technical doctrines forestalling consideration on the merits.

The Supreme Court is, in short, caught in the paradoxical position of striving to appear to apply objective standards in determining not only the necessarily subjective question of the public importance of the legal issues presented in petitions for writ of certiorari, but also in determining whether the time is ripe for judicial resolution of such issues. Should the justices seek to comply with the requests to explain fully the criteria they apply in dealing with certiorari petitions, they would inevitably indicate, or at least open the way for speculation about, the subjective grounds for their actions. Such actions would violate what Justice Harlan recently called "the longstanding and desirable custom of not announcing the conference vote on petitions for certiorari." [16] Under the circumstances it is not surprising that the Supreme Court generally continues to adhere to its policy of reticence. The long-range difficulty with this policy is that its success rests largely on continued public and professional confidence in the Court and its members.

In 1925, at the time that the greatest expansion of the Supreme Court's discretionary authority took place, the Court remained a bastion of economic conservatism. As such it customarily received widespread press support and the dedicated and powerful assistance of professional groups such as the American Bar Association. Social and political changes in the past three decades have altered this situation considerably. As was indicated in Chapter IV, changes in the social role of the Supreme Court have stimulated changes in the attitudes of the leaders of the powerful groups which were once stanch supporters of the Court. The uninhibited attacks of critics of the radical right, such as Rosalie Gordon [17] and David Lawrence, have been paralleled by somewhat more tempered but more effective criticism from conservative bar organizations and newspaper editors. A comprehensive survey of the attitudes on judicial administration of eighty-six newspaper editors representing a cross section of this media was reported to the Section on Judicial Administration of the American Bar Association in the early 1950's. After indicating that many editors had praised areas of improvement in the administration of state and local courts, the report stated,

> There have been 72 editorials critical of [federal] court practices. By far the sharpest criticism has been reserved for the lowered dignity of the Supreme Court of the United States. There have been many bases for these criticisms, which come from every section of the country. The feuding between members of the highest court, their public utterances, their appearance as character witnesses in lower court trials, and the mention of members of the Supreme Court for every sort of job from President to baseball czar have furnished grounds for criticism from every section of the press. *In fact, the press seems a much more active guardian of the lofty dignity of our highest court than its own members.* There seems to be a general feeling among editors that, as the St. Louis Globe-Democrat put it, Justices should "decide now whether they wish to be on the Supreme Court of the United States and add to its deteriorating prestige if they can, or whether they wish to join the larger fraternity of men in public life who profess to have answers to all the questions of politics and diplomacy." [18]

In recent years the strongest attacks upon the Court relating to the initial screening of cases could be found in the publications edited by David Lawrence. Because the clerks of the individual justices conduct a necessarily swift preliminary evaluation of petitions for certiorari, some of the more extreme critics of the Court have charged that clerks with alleged left-wing sympathies have conducted such evaluations on the basis of their ideological inclinations.[19] A number of strong rebuttals by former law clerks have emphasized that the role of the individual clerk is generally so limited in this as well as other aspects of the decision-making process that such intrusions of ideological viewpoints were scarcely likely to occur even if some clerks were ideological activists of some sort. Moreover, every modern judicial biography underscores the intense personal responsibility of the individual justice for every stage of judicial action. The varieties of criticism of the Supreme Court's mode of internal operation are, in themselves, perhaps more indicative of a prevailing change in sentiment in American society than of any serious flaws in the Court's methods of internal procedure. This is not to say that there is no room for economy in judicial effort of the sort recommended recently by Professor Henry M. Hart [20] but that a great deal of the contemporary criticism of internal procedure actually reflects disagreement with the Court's conclusions rather than with its methods of reaching these conclusions.

The Hearing Stage

In the light of Chief Justice Vinson's observation that the cases taken for full consideration under the Supreme Court's discretionary authority were "class actions" involving "tremendously important principles, upon which are based the plans, hopes, and aspirations of a great many people throughout the country," [21] it would seem imperative that every important viewpoint germain to the broad public policy issues raised in such cases be competently presented to the Court. In this context, the question who is permitted to prepare and present written briefs and participate in oral argument is crucial. Willard King's description of the origin of the Income Tax cases of 1895 is illustrative of the fact that on occasion determinative constitutional issues have been settled, at least temporarily, in cases which were privately contrived. King noted that the procedure in the Pollock case was evolved by William D. Guthrie, a young New York lawyer. Certain of his clients wished to contest the constitutionality of the income tax. The usual way to test the validity of a federal tax is to pay it and then sue the collector to get it back. A federal law forbids an injunction against the collection of a tax. Guthrie wished to avoid the delay incident to paying the tax and then suing for it. He therefore raised the issue of the validity of the tax by a suit between private litigants. He had a stockholder of a trust company demand that his company refuse to pay the tax and, upon its declaration of intention to pay despite the demand, sue for an injunction to prevent the corporation from paying the alleged unlawful tax. Guthrie arranged for such a suit to be brought against the Farmers' Loan and Trust Company by a Boston stockholder named Pollock and for a similar suit to be brought against the Continental Trust Company by a New Jersey stockholder named Hyde. Guthrie agreed in advance with the Solicitor General that they should seek a prompt decision in the lower court and take a speedy appeal. As usually is done in such test cases, the trust companies retained a lawyer who was instructed to do everything in his power to sustain the law. The lawyer so engaged was James C. Carter, then one of the ablest men practicing at the bar of the Supreme Court. Guthrie secured Joseph H. Choate as his senior counsel.[22]

It has been sometimes stated that the Income Tax case represents one of the best argued before the Supreme Court.[23] Nevertheless, Carter's deliberate emphasis upon the necessity for the Court to bow to overwhelming public sentiment scarcely seemed keen strategy in light of the strong sentiments publicly expressed by many of the justices for steadfast judicial restraint upon the excesses of democracy.[24] However, leaving aside speculation concerning the intensity or lack of intensity with which arguments against the companies may have been prepared in this instance, it is obvious that such arrangements are not apt to produce the full and spirited treatment of the constitutional issues that would be appropriate to such contests. Further, other situations have arisen where despite the absence of private contrivance the economic resources and hired legal talents evoked by one party far overshadowed the opposition. Yet the legal issues involved had implications of great social import. Perhaps one of the most important procedural devices utilized by the Supreme Court to facilitate competent presentation of viewpoints in crucial cases is found in Supreme Court Rule 42, which permits, under certain circumstances, the submission of *amicus curiae* briefs.

The letter of this rule and the spirit with which it has been applied suggest that the primary objective of the provision of an opportunity for those other than the parties to a case to present arguments is to ensure that important viewpoints not be lost by default or incompetence. A brief of an *amicus curiae* may be presented if all parties to the case give their written consent or, in the event that they refuse, if the Court orders such presentation. Should the parties refuse permission, a motion requesting permission of the Court must "concisely state the nature of the applicant's interest, *set forth the facts or questions of law that have not been,*" or *"reasons for believing that they will not adequately be presented by the parties. . . ."* [25] In recent years, the Court has screened carefully the growing requests for permission to submit *amicus curiae* briefs and has tightened its rules on such matters. Its actions resulted from a growing tendency among some interest groups to utilize this approach to exert pressure on the Court rather than present important viewpoints which were omitted or prepared inadequately in the briefs of the parties to a case.[26] Justice Jackson's criticism of the *amicus curiae* brief submitted by the American Newspaper Publishers Association in *Craig* v. *Harney* is illustrative of the reaction of some members of the Court:

> [The brief] does not cite a single authority not available to counsel for the publisher involved, and does not tell us a single new fact except this one: "This membership embraces more than 700 newspaper publishers whose publications represent in excess of eighty per cent of the total daily and Sunday circulation of newspapers published in this country. The Association is vitally interested in the issue presented in this case, namely, the right of newspapers to publish news stories and editorials on cases pending in the courts." [27]

In addition to the question of who may present arguments, of vital importance is the manner in which such arguments may be presented. Once a case is deemed eligible for consideration on its merits, an opportunity is provided not only for the presentation of what is generally a long written brief but also for oral argument. Despite the fact that the Court has found it necessary, with occasional exceptions, to limit oral arguments to one hour per side, the oral-argument stage is considered of great importance. Indicative of this importance is the fact that Rule 45 states unequivocally that "the court looks with disfavor on the submission of cases on briefs without oral argument, and therefore may, not withstanding such submission, require oral argument by the parties." As Hughes pointed out in his analysis of the Court at work, "a vast amount of time is unavoidably wasted . . . in futile discussion." [28] But the necessity to compress vital arguments may force counsel to dispense with details and unnecessary oratorical excursions. The free and often sharp questioning by the justices is a vital and useful part of the process. Analytical questions, when answered by intelligent counsel, become tools for clarifying issues often hopelessly confused by overly detailed written briefs. Some members of the bar bitterly resent the incisive questioning by the justices. However, without such a practice, it is difficult to conceive of how the oral argument stage would add anything of value to the deliberative process not already provided in the written briefs. After listening to the oral arguments relating to a case, the justices examine systematically the written briefs. Indeed, the written briefs are sometimes read in advance of oral argument. In each case, counsel can assume that all the justices will consider the written brief. The oral argument provides counsel with an opportunity to present to the justices the crucial aspects of the case. If counsel fulfills his role properly in oral argument, he performs a substantial service by assisting the Court in getting to the heart of the matter swiftly; if he performs incompetently, he wastes the Court's valuable time.

The problem of ensuring effective presentation of legal issues of great constitutional import raises long-standing questions about the social significance of the adversary system. Most contemporary lawyers accept the system, and its often very tangible benefits, without serious consideration of its possible broader implications. Some, like Charles P. Curtis, have intelligently evaluated the system and have concluded that, despite its shortcomings, the adversary system should be retained and made more effective.[29] The alternative recommendation, public advocacy, which was seriously mooted by the lawyers of Louis Brandeis' generation, has achieved only limited acceptance in the narrow confines of the embryonic public defender system. Yet the notion that the lawyer may be made primarily an officer of the court(s) and only secondarily a representative of a particular client has had continued vitality, although the specific suggestion of Christian Doerfler that lawyers' "remuneration be derived from the public in the same manner as judges' " [30] was decisively rejected.

The Conference Stage

McElwain's analysis of the manner in which Chief Justice Hughes conducted the business of the Supreme Court has been impressively supplemented by Alpheus T. Mason's judicial biography of Harlan Fiske Stone.[31] Although Hughes and Stone were men quite different in temperament and working habits, the recent treatments by McElwain and Mason underscore the potentially great influence of the chief justiceship upon the decision-making process. As in the past, the modern Court operates in accordance with the institutional tradition that the Chief Justice may in conference first state the issues raised in a case and give his viewpoint on how these issues ought to be resolved. The influence of the Chief Justice is further enhanced by the fact that he chairs the discussion fully as each justice, in descending order of seniority, gives his opinion and observations on the case. After full discussion of a case, the actual vote is taken, this time in reverse order of seniority, the most recently appointed justice voting first, the Chief Justice voting last.

After the voting is completed, the Chief Justice ordinarily undertakes one of the most important tasks, that of assigning the writing of the decision either to himself or to a justice voting with the majority. In the event that the Chief Justice is in dissent, the assignment of the majority opinion is made by the senior associate justice voting with the majority. When the Chief Justice makes the writing assignments, as he does on most occasions, he may apply any criteria he deems important. Marshall tended to assign important decisions to himself in order to enhance the public impression of the unity of the Court. It may be assumed that a similar desire motivated Chief Justice Earl Warren in his writing of the Court's opinion in the Brown case. Indeed, such action has become traditional. In earlier historical eras, the process of case assignment was apparently governed in part by the fact that some of the justices were legal specialists. For example, Thomas Todd was noted for his knowledge of the land laws of the Trans-Appalachian states and Henry Billings Brown for his background in admiralty law.

Perhaps of far greater consequence both historically and in modern times has been the political function performed in the assignment of cases to individual justices. Chief Justice Waite's refusal to assign certain railroad cases to Justice Stephen J. Field was motivated by a desire to prevent damage to the public reputation of the Court.[32] When Chief Justice Taft became convinced that Justice Stone was inclined, ideologically, to align himself with Holmes and Brandeis rather than the conservatives, Taft noticeably cooled on Stone, starting, "I am not always sure how experience as the head of a law school and supervising a law journal helps in making a first class judge." [33] More importantly, Taft's coolness was reflected in the fact that Stone was assigned fewer majority opinions—his majority opinions written in 1929 totaled only seventeen.[34] Mason reports that Chief Justice Hughes tended to assign the writing of highly technical opinions to Stone, whose interest in the Chief Justiceship had been widely discussed before Hughes got the appointment in 1930.[35] In short, the manner in which a Chief Justice performs his case-assigning responsibilities may, in the long run, have an important bearing upon public and professional acceptance or criticism of important decisions, and upon the reputations of the associate justices, some of whom might, on occasion, aspire for promotion to the Chief Justiceship.

In addition to the political function performed by the Chief Justice in the process of assigning the writing chore for each decision, the timing of the assignment of writing obligations has a bearing on the quality of the institutional product. Many state supreme courts follow the practice of rotation of case assignments. Under this system each judge might generally anticipate, before the conference vote, who will have the responsibility for writing the opinion. As Hughes pointed out, each member of the federal Supreme Court "comes to the conference to express his views and to vote, not knowing but that he may have the responsibility of writing the opinion which will accord with the vote. He is thus keenly aware of his responsibility in voting." [36]

In many respects Merlo Pusey's biography of Chief Justice Hughes and Alpheus Mason's biography of Chief Justice Stone [37] provide polar viewpoints on the question of the propriety or impropriety of strong efforts on the part of a Chief Justice to "mass the Court." It is quite clear that Hughes and Stone had quite different conceptions of the proper role of the Chief Justice and that these differences were not merely reflections of variations in temperament but represented deep-seated disagreement over the function of the Conference. For Stone (and his successors), speed in the Conference was secondary to the opportunity for "painstaking consideration by every Justice." [38] Public and particularly professional criticism of the contemporary conduct of the Conference is necessarily centered upon the end products of the Conference, since the Conference itself is always maintained secure from all but the members of the Court. Consequently, much of the contemporary criticism of multiple opinions reflects basic assumptions about the function of the Conference as well as the proper manner of preparing opinions.

The Preparation of Opinions

Perhaps no aspect of the internal operation of the Supreme Court has been subjected to more public and professional criticism in modern times than the practice of recording dissenting and concurring opinions. Members of the legal profession have long been critical of "one-man" decisions in multi-membered appellate courts.[39] Yet, although it has been suggested that dissenting and concurring opinions may be viewed as healthy evidence of the absence of one-man decisions,[40] such opinions have been generally deplored. A strong indication of the intensity of professional opposition to the practice may be found in Canon 19 of the Canons of Judicial Ethics adopted by the American Bar Association:

> It is of high importance that judges constituting a court of last resort should use effort and self-restraint to promote solidarity of conclusion and the consequent influence of judicial decision. A judge should not yield to pride of opinion or value more highly his individual reputation than that of the court to which he should be loyal. Except in case of conscientious difference of opinion on fundamental principle, dissenting opinions should be discouraged in courts of last resort.

The strong contemporary professional antipathy toward full expression of opinions deviating from that of the Court's majority is in part a reflection of the virtually complete victory which advocates of legal conservatism have won in America since the era of Marshall, Story, and Kent. The reluctance toward separate opinions may be deemed one facet of an intellectual movement in American law which succeeded in establishing the ascendency of the common law over civil law,[41] in defeating for long periods the attempts at codification,[42] and in enshrining natural law conceptions while, conversely, rejecting the intellectual challenges of American advocates of Benthamite legal philosophy.[43] The opponents of legal conservatism were not without their great intellectual champions—John Archibald Campbell, David Dudley Field, Edward Livingston, Nicholas St. John Green, and, spanning the nineteenth century into the modern era, Oliver Wendell Holmes. However, until comparatively recent times the main stream of American legal thought was in the conservative tradition.

In this context, the sort of spirited defense of the uses of dissent and of the reversal of hallowed precedents undertaken by Justice William O. Douglas [44] is often viewed in professional circles (omitting some academic reactions) as sheer heresy.[45] What are the intellectual foundations of the conservative legal tradition with respect to the preparation of judicial decisions? The essay on dissenting opinions, written by William A. Bowen in 1905, represents the classic expression of that tradition. Implicit in his analysis were basic assumptions about the ultimate purposes of law. As Bowen put it, "The fundamental security of all peoples lies, not in the *justice,* but in the *certainty,* of their laws." Institutional unity, assumed Bowen, must be maintained in order to create and perpetuate the myth that judges find rather than make law. The use of dissent therefore is unfortunate because such use weakens public acceptance of this myth. In Bowen's words,

> The Dissenting Opinion is of all judicial mistakes the most injurious. Its effect on the public respect for courts is difficult to exaggerate. It is, happily, a habit of the public mind to regard the judiciary as the worthy and safe repository of all legal wisdom; but this respect must receive a sad shock when every court is divided against itself, and every cause reveals the amateurish uncertainty of the judicial mind. . . . The Dissenting Opinion is [most unfortunately] injurious . . . in those cases which are of the greatest public moment. Yet it is the almost unbelievable fact, that it is the uniform justification of dissenting judges that the importance of the case warrants and demands their dissent. . . .
>   . . . Of the many injurious aspects of the Dissenting Opinion, one of the most destructive is that by emphasizing the personal composition of courts it is subversive of their great anonymous authority. . . .
>   . . . The attitude of discussion which the Dissenting Opinion assumes, and the heat of argument which it sometimes evokes, create naturally a tendency to travel far outside the law and to extend the discussion to all manner of subjects, political, social, and economic, and cause the objecting judges to forget that it is not their provénce to make the law, nor even direct its policy, but merely to interpret it.[46]

Bowen's critique of dissent reflects, of course, the self-assurance of conservatives in a simpler age. Modern legal conservatives continue to deplore dissents and the reversal of precedents, but they often omit reference to the argument that the

Court interprets rather than makes law. The modern conservatives indeed have not abandoned the conception as part of the
imagery of an ideal judicial system, but in the face of decision-
making tendencies which they deplore, they prefer not to invoke
the image in behalf of the Warren Court or its post-1937 predecessors. For example, one of Ben Palmer's series of critical articles
in the *American Bar Association Journal* stated,

> If lower court judges, anxious to avoid error, and lawyers with
> the responsibility for advising clients, were baffled by dissent and
> the swirling currents of multiple opinions, they were completely
> confused by the reversal and re-reversal of precedents. . . .[47]

By implication the ideal of judicial interpretation as discovery
rather than creation lay behind criticisms of the modern justices,
who, allegedly, have perverted the uses of judicial power for
political ends. In this vein an *American Bar Association Journal*
editorial commented in 1947 that journalistic criticism such as
David Lawrence's was caused by the appointment of justices who
failed to maintain the Olympian mystery—"men who were not
properly experienced and trained for judicial work and [were
lacking in] the independence, the impartiality and fidelity to the
judicial function which are indispensable." [48]

The liberal legal tradition in America owes an historic debt
to Jeremy Bentham but derives much of its contemporary vitality
from the pragmatism of James and Dewey and the contributions
of jurists such as Holmes and Cardozo and of philosophers such
as Morris Raphael Cohen. A consistent theme throughout the
works of such intellectual contributors is the idea that law, while
it must necessarily be protected against capricious decision making, must be interpreted in the context of each historical era,
that public policy considerations are properly the province of
judges, and that, as a consequence, law must be viewed as subject to change rather than as consisting of immutable principles.
It was Hughes, a great modern practitioner rather than philosopher,
who gave the classic appraisal of the function of dissent in the
context of this liberal tradition:

A dissent in a court of last resort is an appeal to the brooding spirit of the law, to the intelligence of a future day, when a later decision may possibly correct the error into which the dissenting judge believes the court to have been betrayed.[49]

In a somewhat different vein, Justice William O. Douglas stressed the fact that the issues of constitutional law were especially susceptible to intensely differing interpretations. "When judges do not agree, it is a sign that they are dealing with problems on which society itself is divided." Douglas' admonition that judges who "are true to their responsibilities and traditions . . . will not hesitate to speak frankly and plainly on the great issues coming before them" [50] is consistent with the Jeffersonian conception of the role of judges in a democratic society. In contemporary America, however, it is, as was noted above, the conservative tradition of Marshall and Story which finds general approval in the organized bar and among many federal and state judges. And, further, the Jeffersonian emphasis upon the competitive clash of ideas and policy alternatives probably has far less appeal among most members of contemporary American society than among the members of the Supreme Court. Thus the tendency toward full expression of dissent or concurrence has occurred, ironically, in an historic era in which public debate of many fundamental issues has been considered unfashionable or unnecessary.

Carl Brent Swisher, in his perceptive recent work, *The Supreme Court in Modern Role,* has argued that "to the extent of the inability of justices to agree on decisions and on statements of the law, the Court as a whole has failed to complete the performance of its ideal function." This ideal function is, in Swisher's estimation, ultimately the provision of constitutional leadership as "an organic unit." [51] This viewpoint is consistent with the tradition of Court unity associated most notably with John Marshall. But it should be noted that this is not the only viewpoint on this question. The Jeffersonian tradition of frank expression of diverse judicial viewpoints has not, of course, found favor among Supreme Court members in many historic eras for the simple reason that the justices often rejected, implicitly, most facets of Jefferson's political and social thought.

The modern Court has, in effect, chosen to fulfill one of two competing conceptions of the proper role of an appellate tribunal. Whether the choice for all of the justices is deliberate or not is unimportant. It is clear, however, that for some, such as Justice Douglas, it is a deliberate choice made in full knowledge of the fact that diversity in judicial expression is not in accord with either the conservative legal tradition or with the temper of the times. Thus, for Douglas, the ideal judge should not submerge his views in order to achieve institutional unity. In his words,

> We must expect of judges the fortitude and courage that we demand of all other servants who man our public posts. If they are true to their responsibilities and traditions, they will not hesitate to speak frankly and plainly on the great issues coming before them. . . . Their discussion and propagation of the great principles of our Charter may keep the democratic ideal alive in days of regression, uncertainty and despair. . . . [T]heir cool detachment and courageous objectivity can set the fashion of a day and stamp an era with a distinctive character.[52]

It would be a mistake, of course, to attribute the tendency to dissent and concurrence solely to the impact of conceptions of the judicial function entertained by the contemporary justices. The problems attendant to the preparation of opinions are very closely related to those found in the stage of preliminary screening of issues which the Court is urged to consider on their merits. The very fact that the Court now possesses the discretionary power to take none but the most important cases virtually assures that it will consider only legal problems which are most difficult of solution. Consequently, invidious comparisons of the incidence of dissent and concurrence among the federal Supreme Court, the federal Courts of Appeals, and the highest appellate courts of the states overlook the uniqueness of the Supreme Court's role in modern society. Little that is accepted for full consideration by the federal Supreme Court is susceptible to the relatively routine treatment which might serve to create a public image of institutional unity.

Swisher felt that factors related to the modern development of staff assistance to the justices contributed to diversity in opinion writing. Whether or not the clerks and secretaries of the justices invariably develop into "rooting sections" [53] is conjectural. That this possibility existed long before the widespread modern use of dissent and concurrence would suggest, however, that this factor is, of itself, not very decisive.[54] Similarly, there seems to be no necessary relation between personal communication, in person or in writing, between the justices and political and social acquaintances and the degree to which the Court indulges in the writing of multiple opinions. Intense involvement in the mainstream of the intellectual currents of their respective eras was characteristic of many of the justices, as has been attested in numerous judicial biographies. However, the widespread writing of multiple opinions has been characteristic of court practice only in certain eras.

In retrospect, the effect of congressional bestowal of discretionary authority and the impact of several facets of liberal legal philosophy are the most important factors contributing to the free expression of divergent judicial viewpoints. Whether this tendency in decision writing will become as sturdy a judicial tradition in the internal operation of the Supreme Court in the next century as Marshall's tradition of judicial unity was in the past may well be determined by factors operating upon the whole American society.

References

1. Robert L. Stern and Eugene Gressman, *Supreme Court Practice* (2nd ed.; Washington: BNA Incorporated, 1954), pp. 11, 276–292.

2. A four-year total, 1949 through 1952, was 87.6 per cent; Fowler V. Harper and Arnold Leibowitz, "What the Supreme Court Did Not Do during the 1952 Term," *102 University of Pennsylvania Law Review* (1953–1954), 461–462.

3. Joan Maisel Leiman, "The Rule of Four," *57 Columbia Law Review* (1957), 978–982. Although much of the following emphasized the applica-

tion of this rule to certiorari petitions, it should be noted that the rule of four applies with respect to jurisdictional statements on appeal; see Justice Brennan's memorandum in *Ohio ex rel. Eaton* v. *Price,* 360 U.S. 246 (1959).

4. Harold B. Willey, "Jurisdictional Statements on Appeals to U.S. Supreme Court," *31 American Bar Association Journal* (1945), 239.

5. Fowler V. Harper and George C. Pratt, "What the Supreme Court Did Not Do during the 1951 Term," *101 University of Pennsylvania Law Review* (1952–1953), 454–479.

6. Fowler V. Harper and Alan S. Rosenthal, "What the Supreme Court Did Not Do in the 1949 Term," *99 University of Pennsylvania Law Review* (1950–1951), 293; Harper and Edwin D. Etherington, "What the Supreme Court Did Not Do during the 1950 Term," *100 University of Pennsylvania Law Review* (1951–1952), 354; Harper and Pratt, *loc. cit.,* p. 439; and Harper and Leibowitz, *loc. cit.,* p. 427.

7. *Brown* v. *Allen,* 344 U.S. 497 (1953); italics mine.

8. *Ibid.,* p. 542.

9. Ernest J. Brown, "The Supreme Court: 1957 Term," *72 Harvard Law Review* (1958–1959), 81.

10. Rule 19, *Revised Rules of the Supreme Court* (1954).

11. Harper and Leibowitz, *loc. cit.,* pp. 427–435.

12. Stern and Gressman, *op. cit.,* p. 157.

13. Quoted in *ibid.,* pp. 107–108.

14. The Court could, of course, answer that the erroneous decisions selected involved issues of national significance.

15. Dissent in *Ferguson* v. *Moore–McCormack Lines, Inc.,* 352 U.S. 528 (1957).

16. Dissent in *Ferguson* v. *Moore–McCormack Lines, Inc.,* 352 U.S. 561 (1957).

17. See, for example, Rosalie Gordon, *Nine Men against America: The Supreme Court and Its Attack on American Liberties* (New York: The Devin–Adair Company, 1958).

18. Report by James J. Kerney, Jr., editor of the *Trenton* (New Jersey) *Times,* to the American Bar Association's Committee on Co-operation with Laymen of the Section on Judicial Administration, September 19, 1951, Waldorf–Astoria Hotel, New York City, N.Y., pp. 31–32; italics mine.

19. See the legislative and investigative recommendations of Senator John Stennis, "Investigate Supreme Court Law Clerk System?" *United States News and World Report* (May 16, 1958). Stennis quoted approvingly the allegations made by William H. Rehnquist in *United States News and World Report* (December 13, 1957).

20. I refer specifically to his criticism of the policy of granting certiorari in Federal Employer's Liability Act cases, Henry M. Hart, Jr., "Foreword: The Time Chart of the Justices," *73 Harvard Law Review* (1959–1960), 96–97.

21. See note 9, above.

22. Willard King, *Melville Weston Fuller* (New York: The Macmillan Company, 1950), p. 194.

23. John P. Frank refers to the tradition that the two greatest arguments were made in the Dartmouth College and Income Tax cases, *Marble Palace* (New York, Alfred A. Knopf, Inc., 1958), p. 87.

24. See, for example, the address by Justice Brewer, "The Movement of Coercion," to the New York State Bar Association on January 17, 1893; *16 Proceedings of the New York State Bar Association* (1893), 37–47.

25. Section 3 of Rule 42; italics mine.

26. For a full discussion, see Clement E. Vose, "Litigation as a Form of Pressure Group Activity," *Annals of the American Academy of Political and Social Science,* CCCXIX (1958).

27. Jackson wrote here in dissent; 331 U.S. 397 (1946).

28. Charles Evans Hughes, *The Supreme Court of the United States* (New York: Garden City Books, 1928), p. 61.

29. See Charles P. Curtis, *It's Your Law* (Boston: Little Brown & Company, 1954), pp. 1–5.

30. Christian Doerfler, "The Duty of the Lawyer as an Officer of the Court," *24 Green Bag* (1912).

31. Edwin McElwain, "The Business of the Supreme Court as Conducted by Chief Justice Hughes," *63 Harvard Law Review* (1949–1950), Alpheus T. Mason, *Harlan Fiske Stone: Pillar of the Law* (New York: The Viking Press, Inc., 1956).

32. See Chapter 5 of this book, pp. 120–121.

33. Mason, *op. cit.,* p. 260.

34. *Ibid.*

35. *Ibid.,* pp. 316–317.

36. Hughes, *op. cit.,* p. 59.

37. Merlo J. Pusey, *Charles Evans Hughes* (2 vols.; New York: The Macmillan Company, 1951), and Mason, *op. cit.*

38. Mason, *op. cit.,* p. 575.

39. See Justice John Hessin Clarke's answer to this criticism in "How the U.S. Supreme Court Works," *9 American Bar Association Journal* (1923), 81.

40. Laurance M. Hyde (chairman), "Report of a Committee to Gather Information Concerning Methods of Reaching and Preparing Appellate Court Decisions." Presented to the Section of Judicial Administration, Annual Meeting of the American Bar Association, August, 1942, p. 32.

41. For an interesting example of the intensity of the intellectual struggle, see Justice John A. Campbell's comments about the judicial reasoning of Justice Joseph Story in his dissent in *Jackson* v. *Steamboat Magnolia,* 20 Howard 296 (1857).

42. See the biographical accounts of the codification efforts of Edward Livingston and David Dudley Field.

43. John R. Schmidhauser, "Jeremy Bentham, the Contract Clause and

Justice John Archibald Campbell," *11 Vanderbilt Law Review* (1957–1958).

44. See, for example, William O. Douglas, "The Dissent: A Safeguard of Democracy," *32 Journal of the American Judicature Society* (December, 1948), p. 104, and his "Stare Decisis," *49 Columbia Law Review* (1949), 735.

45. Ben W. Palmer's comments may be viewed as typical of much of the legal profession; see note 47.

46. William A. Bowen, "Dissenting Opinions," *17 Green Bag* (1905), 690–697.

47. Ben Palmer, "Dissents and Overrulings," *34 American Bar Association Journal* (1948), 556.

48. *33 American Bar Association Journal* (1947), 150.

49. Hughes, *op. cit.*, p. 68.

50. Douglas, *loc. cit.*, pp. 104–105.

51. Carl Brent Swisher, *The Supreme Court in Modern Role* (New York: New York University Press, 1958), pp. 180–181.

52. Douglas, *loc. cit.*, pp. 106–107.

53. Swisher, *op. cit.*, p. 188.

54. For evidence that such tendencies were operative in the 1880's, see Samuel Williston's autobiographical account, *Law and Life* (Boston: Little, Brown & Company, 1941), pp. 86–101.

—— IV

Conclusions

7

An Over-All Appraisal

THE FACTORS discussed in the preceding five chapters by no means exhaust the catalogue of subtle influences which condition the decision-making process of the Supreme Court. These have been stressed because they have, in the opinion of the writer, been of special significance for the post-1937 Court. To the question what sort of combination of such factors comprises a predictable explanation for specific decision-making behavior, the answer necessarily is inconclusive. The inconclusiveness of this answer need not, however, discourage further investigations of judicial behavior of the sort employing associational statistical or related methods. Rather, it may serve at once as a caution against oversimplification and as a challenge to more intense yet sensitive effort.

In the final analysis, the relative importance of such factors as ideological outlook, social and political background, or institutional tradition may well be governed by certain personal attributes of the individuals who have served on the Court. Understanding and appreciation of the intellectual value of the deliberative process might well rank high among such attributes. In this respect the capability for adaption to the institutional demands of service on the Court—both intellectual and with regard to style of living—would be crucial.

Judgments concerning this capability of individual justices entail necessary evaluations of the quality of their judicial work. Such evaluations are, as was indicated in Chapter IV, often based upon subjective considerations closely related to approval or disapproval of the ideological values of the justices. Consequently, it is extremely difficult to divorce assessment of the quality of judicial endeavor from such considerations. However, the biographical data, if treated with sensitivity to this problem, do contain important insights which permit the making of certain tentative conclusions.

Although overly eulogistic chroniclers of the Supreme Court, such as Hampton Carson, have tended to create a negative attitude toward excessive praise of the justices, it is of course true that in virtually every historical period men like Marshall, William Johnson, Taney, Curtis, Campbell, Miller, Field, Bradley, Holmes, Hughes, Stone, Brandeis, and Cardozo, regardless of their ideological attachments, have generally and justifiably been recognized as "great" judges. In the context of the particular requirements of service on the Supreme Court, the attainment of greatness has usually been based upon a combination of personal qualities such as political sagacity (frequently called judicial statesmanship), high intellectual ability (but not necessarily philosophic training or detachment), and a flair for literary accomplishment.[1] Learning in the law, in its more profound sense, like a penchant for legal philosophy, was not universal among the great judges. Some, like Marshall and Miller, frequently had to depend upon others to develop the legal researches necessary to the justification of the judicial policies which they sought to establish. The influence of the truly great judges on the Supreme Court cannot be measured simply in terms of the decisions they handed down. The impact of their personalities may be found in the subtle fashioning of the internal procedures and customs of the Court and in the scattered biographical evidences of their masterful understanding of the manipulative potentialities in small group situations.

The majority of the justices were not great judges but clearly were individuals of more than average ability and legal training who conscientiously fulfilled their duties with vigor and high intelligence. In some instances, members in this category made contributions, such as exhaustive research in fields such as patent law, admiralty law, or the land laws of certain states, which were important to the balanced fulfillment of the Supreme Court's obligations. Justices Story and Gray were outstanding examples of this class of justice.

Tragic for the nation and for the individuals themselves were the members who must be categorized as mediocre. In virtually every historical period a few men have been appointed to the Supreme Court who lacked the intellectual capacity and breadth of vision to carry the responsibilities of decision making with ability or composure. Yet because of the prestige which attached to such appointments, the mediocre clung as tenaciously to their positions as their more able colleagues. The result of such appointments was usually trying for the better justices—the abler justices either had to endure the poorly written and weakly reasoned decisions of the mediocre or had to assume the added burden of cases which the mediocre could not handle adequately. The poorly qualified justices themselves either lapsed into crabbed laziness (as has been charged concerning Justice McReynolds) [2] or laboriously eked out decisions of poor quality.

The biographical material on Justice Nathan Clifford etches a clear picture of a hard-working justice who, because of his determination to continue to fill a position for which he lacked the highest ability, sacrificed all opportunity for recreation and relaxation for a period of over two decades. In the words of his grandson,

> Nathan was not brilliant. . . . He possessed the ability for hard work and the slow, plodding retentive mind. . . .
>
> The tasks before him had to be done, and were faithfully and laboriously accomplished without apparent thought of anything else.[3]

In a similar vein, Matthew McDevitt, biographer of Justice McKenna, wrote,

> [McKenna was] regarded as somewhat slow in his mental processes, confused in his logic and lacking in easily definable legal philosophy. . . . During his twenty-seven years on the bench Justice McKenna led a secluded and retired life. Although invited to numerous social functions he refused to accept lest he be deprived of the time which he believed should be devoted to his

heavy court duties. He could invariably be found at his desk in his study from eight o'clock in the morning and after dinner in the evening, until in his later years, when poor eyesight compelled him to forgo night work. . . . He bestowed the same care and industry on the insignificant as on controversies of pivotal import.[4]

The psychological effect of mediocrity upon the Court as a social institution is rather difficult to assess, but the impact of a justice's recognition of his own inadequacy could have far-reaching consequences for the sensitive small group relations which comprise so great a part of the Court's internal operations. The following biographical materials taken from McDevitt provide a striking illustration of the possibilities inherent in such situations:

> In his early years on the bench, he [McKenna] was frequently irritable, nervous and rather unhappy because he was not familiar with the law nor *able to construct an opinion that would adequately express the convictions of his colleagues.* . . . McKenna cautiously felt his way and although his ideas were strong and forceful, yet he rarely struck out on an original line of thought. He anchored his deductions on authority and filled the pages of his opinions with numerous references and a monotonous series of diffuse and uncritical quotations. With passing years, he became more certain of his ability, and his expressions were characterized by greater breadth and independence of thought. *He became increasingly assertive of his own views until his self-assuredness almost amounted to impatience with the conclusions of others.*[5]

The prime safeguard against mediocrity is acute sensitivity to the problem in the appointing authority. With respect to the contemporary scene, there clearly is little indication that the acceptance of the advice of interested private groups with respect to judicial appointments provides any greater assurance against mediocrity than has the traditional political process.

In many respects, the prospects for the retention by the Supreme Court of its unique place in the American political process may depend more on developments which are external to the Court than on those which are a part of its institutional character. Perhaps the most important of these developments is the erosion, since 1937, of the traditional support accorded the Supreme Court by conservative private associations. This support was generally forthcoming because the Supreme Court, in fulfilling its constitutional role as defender of minority rights against oppression by the majority, emphasized the Hamiltonian insistence upon the protection of the rights of property. The question for the future is whether the modern judicial tendency to emphasize human noneconomic rights will eventually attract sufficient support for the Court to replace the conservative interests which were so important in the past.

References

1. The criteria for greatness in judicial service which are applied here resemble in certain respects the standards adopted by Charles Fairman and Anthony Lewis but also deliberately eschew several. For example, concern for getting facts and disinterestedness (included by Fairman and Lewis, respectively) were not noticeable attributes of the judicial career of either Marshall or Miller; yet few would omit either man from the roster of great judges. See Charles Fairman, "What Makes a Great Justice: Mr. Justice Bradley and the Supreme Court, 1870–1892," *30 Boston University Law Review* (1950), 49–102; and Anthony Lewis, "What Qualities for the Supreme Court?" *New York Times Magazine,* October 6, 1957, p. 100.

2. Justice Holmes wrote to Pollock on one occasion: "On Monday next we sit again, I shall have an opinion and three dissents to pass off— two opinions held up, one for McReynolds to make up his mind about, the other for him to write a dissent. He takes his time, which I must confess gets on my nerves. . . ." Letter of April 4, 1928; Mark DeWolfe Howe (ed.), *Holmes-Pollock Letters,* II (Cambridge, Mass.: Harvard University Press, 1941), 218.

3. Philip Greeley Clifford, *Nathan Clifford, Democrat* (New York: G. P. Putnam's Sons, 1922), pp. 5, 331.

4. Matthew McDevitt, *Joseph McKenna, Associate Justice of the United States* [sic] (Washington: Catholic University Press, 1946), pp. 225–226.

5. *Ibid.,* pp. 202–203.

Index